FAMINE IN ENGLAND

FAMINE
IN ENGLAND

By

VISCOUNT LYMINGTON

SPECIAL EDITION FOR
THE "RIGHT" BOOK CLUB
10 SOHO SQUARE, LONDON W.1

First published 1938
Reprinted for the " Right " Book Club 1938

19716

H. F. & G. WITHERBY LTD.
326 HIGH HOLBORN, LONDON W.C.I
MADE IN GREAT BRITAIN
PRINTED BY SHERRATT & HUGHES, ST. ANN'S PRESS
TIMPERLEY, CHESHIRE·

PREFACE

Had it not been for the urgency of the situation in England, this book would not have been attempted by the writer at a few months' notice.

To diagnose our faults is necessary if we are to cure them. The attack on entrenched positions has not been made to shock or amuse but to evoke a true understanding of the magnitude of our difficulties in the hope that by this understanding we may grasp the necessity for a philosophy which places first the livelihood of good men living for and by the living earth. The first part of this book makes grim reading for that very reason. Those who agree already that there is a danger of war and that without food reserves and a full use of the land there is danger of famine and revolution, need not linger over the first three chapters. But while these chapters show the urgency of an agricultural revival, the chapter on the still unfamiliar spectacle of world erosion and waste of land is designed to emphasize the importance of a long view for home agriculture, just as the chapter on our subnormal state of health is designed to give to a regenerate agriculture a new meaning in statesmanship. In the last half of the book dealing with the constructive side of agriculture, the emphasis is thrown on the health of the soil even more than on quick production from the soil, since on this alone can the health of our people depend, and by this alone can we hope for ultimate safety from the new deserts under which man may bury the " Progress " he has created.

So in spite of its imperfection in expression and in spite of the hasty compression and omissions which the size of the volume enforces, the writer makes no apology for its publication. The writer is aware that there are many exceptions to his strictures, at home and in the Empire. But these are the exceptions upon which we could build a regenerate nation, if we acknowledge that it is not speculation and usury which matters in commerce but exchange to mutual advantage. Exchangers are less important than producers, and among producers it is those who till the soil upon whom civilization is based, more than upon those who mine or manufacture. This has been forgotten in Europe and America, and the standards of the speculator, and the mass manufacturer have taken the place of the standard of the husbandman.

We in Britain have forgotten this for longer than any other country and our position is on that account the worse. We must adjust ourselves to reality and understand that without so doing war can bring immediate disaster. It is indeed the personal responsibility of everyone who can understand the danger to urge his leaders to act.

May those who read discern the signposts here and turn while there is still a fairway to be found; because

> " I tell the things I know, the things I knew
> Before I knew them, immemorially." [1]

[1] V. Sackville-West, *The Land*, p. 4.

CONTENTS

9

ACKNOWLEDGMENTS

I T is impossible to make acknowledgments to the teachers from whom the thought in this book has slowly grown. Many of them, indeed, are the wise and almost inarticulate servants of the soil itself.

More than formal acknowledgments are due to Mr. J. F. Murphy, Secretary in the Department of Commerce, Canberra, for his assistance in providing information as to erosion in Australia. This information, while not quoted in detail, was of the greatest value in writing Chapter VI. Likewise, the author is greatly indebted to the courtesy and help of Dr. Marsden and his assistants in the department of Scientific and Industrial Research of New Zealand, on the question of erosion.

The assistance of Mr. G. Brown, of the National Farmers' Union staff at 45 Bedford Square, the officials of the Farmers' Club, and the officials of the Ministry of Agriculture, has been invaluable.

Acknowledgments are also due to the U.S. Department of Agriculture (Bureau of Agriculture and Economics); The Navy League; The

Bankers' Institute; The Petroleum Press Service; The International Institute of Agriculture, Rome; The International Superphosphate Manufacturers' Association; The Swiss Bank Corporation; H.M. Stationery Office for permission to quote the graph and statistics on pp. 218–22, 224, from the Agricultural Statistics of 1934 and 1935; also for permission to quote from the Table accompanying BR. 84; Sir Robert McCarrison, C.I.E., M.D., D.Sc., LL.D., F.R.C.P., for permission to quote from the Gabriel Howard Memorial Lecture of 1937; Mrs. Rudyard Kipling and Messrs. Macmillan & Co., publishers, for permission to quote the extract from " The Mother Hive " in *Actions and Reactions* at the beginning of Part I; The Imperial Economic Committee for permission to quote from Dairy Produce Supplies 1936.

Finally, thanks are due to Baron de Rutzen for his untiring help in the preparation of statistical information and the work of checking this in the manuscript.

TO THOSE WHO
LABOUR ON THE LAND
AND SERVE IT

PART I

War

Now panic was in full blast, and each sound bee found herself embraced by at least three Oddities. The first instinct of a frightened bee is to break into the stores and gorge herself with honey; but there were no stores left, so the Oddities fought the sound bees. "You must feed us, or we shall die!" they cried, holding and clutching and slipping, while the silent scared earwigs and little spiders twisted between their legs. "Think of the Hive, traitors! The Holy Hive!" "You should have thought of that before!" cried the sound bees. "Stay and see the dawn of your New Day."

RUDYARD KIPLING, *The Mother Hive*

CHAPTER I

WAR

STARVING mariners have been known to dice in the sporting tradition for the privilege of not being eaten by their fellows. But hungry bellies command no niceties and respect no rules or persons; so in practice it is generally the lot of the cabin-boy to be the first meal in the ultimate ration. When a nation starves there is no quarter, and no discrimination.

If one considers the neglected fields and the teeming population of these islands, a starving nation is no fantastic vision but an ever-present possibility. Eight millions were reckoned to have died of famine not two decades past in Russia, where land was almost limitless. Starvation has left scars on Germany and Austria and parts of Eastern Europe from the last war that are still unhealed; starvation brought Germany to her knees and gave her over to revolution and civil war; yet Germany was far more self-supporting than we could hope to be at present, for in 1914 she produced 85 per cent. of her food requirements.[1] Starvation is the advance guard of panic, disease

[1] For the appalling effect of our blockade on the civil population of Germany, in tuberculosis, infant and maternal mortality, death-rate, and the increase of morbidity, see " The Report on Food Conditions in Germany ", by Ernest R. Starling, C.M.G., M.D., F.R.S. (Cmd. 280) 1919.

and civil war. It is the herald of the new dark ages. If starvation halted armies, goaded men to revolution, and altered maps in the peasant lands of Europe after one war, what can it help but do to Britain, without food for half her people or means to import it? This is what war means to us.

Who can deny that the appetites of other nations and the follies of our own foreign policy have not brought war very near in the last two years? War over Abyssinia, war over Spain, war with Germany. Few want it, but in a military writer's phrase " war comes like a shooting star ". It comes in this fashion for two reasons : lack of fixity in purpose, lack of means to pursue any purpose. And when both these reasons are present sooner or later a war is almost inevitable. The statesman who babbles of only fighting a war of defence is guilty of the gravest betrayal of those whom he seeks to guide and rule. In such circumstances a war of defence can only mean a war of defencelessness because the attack will come at the enemies' choice.

War is a dangerous instrument of policy and none desire it save for overwhelming reasons. Thus a war of ruthless and calculated aggression at a chosen moment is the only one which can be justified to a nation. The only sane alternative is to guard a position so strong that no one will dare to attack. There is always the qualification that a nation may have to fight to the death against an attack by a country temporarily hysterical, or through being involved in a religious crusade or a great cataclysm of racial upheaval. Yet even these chances the wise ruler with fixity of purpose should foresee and be prepared to forestall. It is outside the scope of this book to survey the possibilities of a yellow race war or a Jehad in the renascent Islam of to-day. Suffice to say that these exist and that our foreign policy has been such as to aggravate those possibilities, if Britain is weak or becomes involved in a European war through lack of purpose. We are in a very grave position in India, where our arrogant policy of westernizing an ancient civilization has handed India over to the lawyer, the moneylender, and the terrorist; while our weakness, physical and moral, has opened the way for terror and disintegration. Trouble for Britain in India is the communists' desire. It is Japan's opportunity. Likewise our Palestinian policy is rousing not only the native Arab, but is estranging our Mohammedan subjects and one time friends from Kenya to Bengal. It is the stuff from which new Jehads can be made.

Neither the yellow races nor Islam would be sorry to see a European war which brought them nearer to recovering mastery of the world. A weakened England would be for them of all things most desirable. The Empire, which, in a dead patriot's phrase is " the greatest block of undefended plunder the world has ever seen ", would fall like ripe plums into their hands.

Another danger in Europe is a league of nations

which upholds the *litera scripta* of Versailles. The minority question all over Central Europe makes it a political earthquake zone. Any one outbreak may cause a European war. Those who have gained all over Europe will join to keep their gains; those who have lost will jump into the vortex to take their chance. At present we are powerless to prevent it or to keep from fighting ourselves. Popular opinion can often be fomented to cause war in any country by the skilful manipulation of those who hope to gain nationally or internationally. Strength of arm and security of supply alone can give us the means of keeping out of war or preventing a conflagration. Jenkin's ears and Don Pacificos are still in fashion, when it suits the pacifists. Passionate devotion to the Red Ensign is shown immediately it floats over foreign crews and red gun-runners, however much it is dishonoured by these same people when it upholds British interests.

There is another danger by which world war is encouraged: the Communist genuinely believes that only a proletarian revolution will save the world. The destruction of white civilization is for him the hope of world unity; therefore to the Communist war is to be welcomed. After war comes dissolution and the break up of the old order. International Communist propaganda is accordingly as much devoted to fomenting trouble between nations as it is to fomenting class war. It is for this reason that the self-sufficiency of sovereign states like Germany and Italy, the service of race and soil, is in his eyes a menace. There may be many reasons why we dislike the internal government of these two states, but they are not the Communist reasons; to the Communist the service of race and soil means the retention of the old ethnic order. Hence propaganda using international idealism through Geneva and the self-justification of world finance, is most often directed against nationalism.

England has suffered since the war from professional pacifists. Some few are doubtless pure in heart. Your jingo pacifist is only the tool of revolutionaries who wish to create war. Any dictatorship by the right whatever its benefits and however much welcomed and accepted by the nation in which it occurs, is something to be wiped out. Tyranny and wholesale slaughter by the left is discreetly forgotten.

Italy may be a menace to our Eastern communications, the virility of Germany may loom ominous to our politicians, but war against either would be suicidal. Yet the final end of such propaganda and a policy which links us to Russia via France may all too easily mean that war will come "like a shooting star". The average Englishman would like to see a prosperous, healthy and friendly Germany, and save for his lines of communication doesn't care whether Mussolini or the Amhara tribe is master of Abyssinia. But the endless propaganda directed in a sinister way against selected Dictatorships in Europe is beginning to make

Germans and Italians believe that we have a consuming hatred of them. These are the media in which the bacteria of war are cultivated, and if these countries believe that they will have to fight us, they will fight far more readily if they consider us weak than if we are strong. The object of this book is to show how we may regain the real strength of our people, and so cease to fear war. Then we may learn how to enjoy peace. But, gloomy though it may be, we must first of all analyse the present dangerous conditions before we can form constructive remedies. So it is necessary to assay the chances of famine before we propose heroic measures to avert them.

CHAPTER II

HUNGER

In war famine is the first danger, but it is only a logical climax to lack of purpose and decision. Famine is one part of the lack of means to pursue a purpose which could save us from a war not of our own choosing. We are repairing the defences in material and partially in skilled and trained men. But lack of food and fuel makes us utterly dependent on others. When a retiring statesman speaks of the essential dignity of the individual soul, he is assuming conditions which hardly exist for us. Essential dignity is not an ideal endowment of all human beings at birth; it comes when men have hope and act with faith and purpose for their families and their nation. There is no necessary dignity in living for a human being any more than there is for a tapeworm. There is dignity in a constructive and purposeful life. Thus men in general only get the Government of which they are worthy. A nation aware of its dangers may save itself; we must understand the danger before we can move to avert it. We must not only see why famine must be inevitable in war, we must see the consequences of famine; it is only the strong who cannot be forced to fight. While we are dependent on food from abroad no amount of armament or pious belief in collective security can make us strong and in any way independent. If there is any danger at all of war occurring, then there must be a danger of famine.

We rely on imported foodstuffs to the tune of one million pounds worth per day; it comes over 85,000 miles of trade routes, sometimes in tramp steamers, sometimes in specially constructed refrigerator vessels.[1] Wheat, beef, mutton and dairy produce come in large quantities from Australia and New Zealand, a distance of over 11,000 miles, even supposing that in war time the Panama Canal was open to us; one quick raid or even American neutrality might close the Panama Canal to us for the whole war. Argentina sends fifty million pounds worth of staple food from 6000 miles away. Our nearest possible source upon which we could rely is Canada, which is 3000 miles away, and Canada's crops are failing. We could put no reliance on Europe. However friendly Scandinavia might be, any European war might involve the Baltic countries or at least prevent them exporting food to us. Denmark, which might in some cases be relied on for bacon and butter, could only feed us by importing, as she does now, animal foodstuffs from the new world. If our supplies were to be cut off from there, so in all probability would hers be cut off. To rely on wheat and maize from the

[1] See Appendix showing sources of food supplies and raw materials.

Danube Valley would be out of the question. Later on it will be shown that, even with a strict reserve of cereals to last a year, our position would be precarious unless home agriculture were in good heart. So far as we know the most optimistic estimate of cereal food reserves now in Britain is a three months' supply. In the months of September, October and November we have a two months' home-grown supply, largely used now for chicken feed and biscuit-making. It is improbable that we would have more than six weeks, and very likely that we would have only three weeks' cereal reserve. In the last decades the growing practice of grain traders is to keep their reserves at sea and divert the grain ships to home or foreign ports as the demand arises. About 1928 there were sufficient warehouses to hold nearly one year's supply of grain at home. An unknown but very large number of these have been converted to other uses. One of the main reasons for this has been the gradual squeezing out of all the inland and country millers by the big combines of importers. Thus we are not only defenceless in regard to food reserves, we are defenceless through our inability to store these reserves in sufficient quantity, and such reserves as we could at present store would be vulnerable, since the grain elevators and storehouses are built near the seaports in order to economize labour in unloading from ships. In all our previous wars there was no danger from the air; now the chief aerial dangers are to the East Coast ports from London to

Aberdeen. Relatively speaking, all ports of Britain are vulnerable to attack by sea and by air. Thus not only are present reserves very small, but they are concentrated in the danger points of attack both from sea and air.

It is as well at this point to consider aerial danger to this country. The danger from gas bombing and aerial bombardment generally has probably been grossly exaggerated, although it is none the less a possibility with which to reckon. Few invaders by air would therefore waste time in indiscriminate bombardment, when they could attain their objects of destroying national morale equally well by concentrating on points of military importance, which include first and foremost all the nerve-centres of distribution which lie close at hand. Denmark, Germany, France, Holland and Belgium lie opposite our vulnerable nerve-centres. Long-range bombing does not to-day entirely exclude Russia, Poland, Czechoslovakia, Scandinavia, or even Italy, and any one of these countries might find a forward base by conquest or alliance with countries lying on or close to the North Sea. Moreover, we cannot rule out the possibility of trouble in Ireland and consequent danger to Bristol, Cardiff, Liverpool and Glasgow. Thus nothing short of overwhelming superiority such as a two- or three-power standard in the air could guarantee our protection even in a short war. In a long war air machines are capable of being turned out in large quantities, and no one could guarantee from time to time that mechanical superiority in the air might not change hands. Airmen and infantry alike knew this to their cost in the last war. In addition, we are probably the only considerable country, except Japan, whose nerve-centres of import could, by being paralysed, reduce the whole nation to paralysis. Most of the great nations are self-supporting in food and clothing, many in inland manufactures, and many are better off in oil, fuel oil substitutes, and reserves than ourselves.

We need first of all well over half our supplies of food from abroad. We rely entirely for our Army, Air Force and Navy as well as for half our commercial shipping, on oil fuel. To-day much of our inland transport and our prime movers use oil products. Our home-produced oil fuel is negligible. We are told that we are increasing our home reserves of oil fuel. There is no overt sign of inland oil reserves as yet. Port oil reserves are even more vulnerable to air attack than port grain elevators, because the incendiary bomb would probably ignite heavy oil. Even if we had oil reserves for the Forces for one year adequately protected in inland and underground storage, what is going to happen to industry and transport which is equally vital to the nation in war time? Munitions and clothing will still have to be made, merchant ships supplied, lorries and petrol engines will still have to function at home. Mechanization of land forces, an oil-fired Navy, and of necessity an oil-using Air Force will place such a drain on war-time merchant shipping

27

that the Navy and Air Force will have no time to do anything but guard this position.

Oil supplies may be difficult to obtain. The British Empire supplies are only a small fraction of world output and lie very far afield. The Mosul pipe-line which comes to the sea at the nearest point to England of all our oil supplies, namely Palestine, was thrice cut by Arab bands in 1936, with 40,000 British troops holding Palestine. Enemy raiders will very naturally concentrate on food ships and tankers in distant waters. As tankers are a special type of ship, replacement will not be easy, but by their build they are easy targets to distinguish. Moreover, as most of our potential enemies are also highly mechanized, there will be great competition for neutral tankers and neutral oil supplies,[1] which may be the death-blow to our chances of survival. An America or Mexico in the throes of communism, for instance, would not be likely to supply us in war time.

The oil-fuel question is intimately bound up with the danger of famine in England, since the Navy and Air Force will have to concentrate on keeping open two essential types of supplies in far greater quantities than the one essential type, namely food-stuffs, which were necessary in the last war. This does not mean to say that we will not need munitions, raw material and clothing from abroad, but by converting all our forces and many industrial

[1] The price of oil rose to £15 per ton at the end of the last war.

concerns to reliance on oil fuel since 1918, we have vastly added to our task in keeping open lines of communications.[1] We imported 12,000,000 tons of oil in 1936 as against 2,500,000 in 1914; even our merchant fleet is half oil-fired. This only includes the Navy's peace-time ration for oil, which is probably 10 per cent. of its war-time needs.[2]

The position of our sea routes may be considerably worse if we become embroiled with any major Mediterranean power. Then the only safe route to the East must lie around the Cape of Good Hope; this means more oil and more shipping will be required.

Thus we see that communications are more dangerous than at any time since the Battle of Trafalgar. But the need for open communications has increased literally a hundredfold since then. If our need for oil fuel and other vital imports to supply our services and factories is so urgent, our home food position is equally desperate. Munitions are the material of war, but food is the munition of life. On the quality of our food will depend the quality of our endurance. That is why pestilence follows war. The fatal casualties of the last war were probably less than those in the one winter of 1918–19 from influenza because an ill-nourished world had no resistance to disease. So we must look

[1] See Lord Alwyn's speech, House of Lords Report for June 16th, 1937.
[2] The Navy is only allowed twelve weeks' supply of oil for *cruising at economical speeds* in peace-time each year.

at our food supplies as not only the means to exist, but to give us heart to work and fight well and to resist disease, which is a greater enemy to nations at war than explosives, gas or cold steel. We could exist on half rations of white bread and tinned food for a time. But the heart would be taken out of the nation, since fresh food is the munition for strong bodies. What is our ability to obtain these in time of war? We are importing annually some 600,000 more tons of meat and several hundred thousands more tons of wheat and flour, butter, cheese, vegetables and fruit than in 1914, and our population is increased by more than 3,500,000 souls. Our agriculture at home produces no more of vital supplies save sugar, vegetables and fruit. We produce less beef and mutton, but more milk and bacon. On the other hand our imports of animal foodstuffs have vastly increased and so our home production on balance has declined.

It has been pointed out above that our grain reserves are less than in 1914. The shipping position is infinitely more serious. British shipping is less by over one million tons than in 1914, but shipping registered in the British Isles is less by 1,700,000 tons as the Dominion shipping has increased. More serious still is the size of the ships we now have to rely on under our flag. The average ocean tramp now built is 6000 tons as against 3000 in 1914. Thus we are nearly twice as vulnerable as before, since each ship sunk or disabled means a far heavier loss of carrying

capacity. Also from the point of view of importing fresher and healthier food supplies we require
special ships with refrigerating plants to carry beef,
butter, fruit, and vegetables. Many of these are
large liners; again not only a vulnerable target, but
also the type of ship which will be most needed for
transport and military services. Thus there is no
comfort to be found anywhere in our overseas food
position. The present state of British agriculture
will be shown in a later chapter to be sadly inferior
in fertility to 1914. Suffice to say that in 1914 the
old-fashioned sound type of mixed farming had
left great stores of fertility in the soil which enabled
home agriculture primarily to save our food position in 1915, '17 and '18. The war exhausted
those stocks of fertility and we have never replaced
them, so we are not in a position now to do what
we did then. Moreover, the better part of a million acres of good land has since then been handed
over to the builder and the road-maker, aerodromes, golf-courses, etc. Another million acres
has gone to wilderness, which is called rough grazing or land gone out of cultivation in the official
returns. Thus we are not only less able to import
easily than in 1914; but also we are less able now
to feed ourselves, and our population has increased.

Many who should know better blandly declare
that if our mercantile marine is weaker we have the
other increased merchant navies of the world on
which to rely. But, because the last war meant an
alliance of the whole naval world against Germany,

it is the height of folly to hope for such luck a second time. It is more than likely that at least two great naval powers will be against us. Quite apart from Germany and Italy, whom most of the Press and the peace balloters seemed to want us to fight, an enemy France turned temporarily communist is no impossibility. In any case, many neutrals may be chary of risking their ships and their status with our enemies to send us supplies for non-dated cheques. The international debts of the last war are still largely unhonoured. Indeed, they are unpayable save by ruining the creditor nations. Already the U.S.A. has declared against repeating the policy of her 1914–17 neutrality, when she inflated her industries to export to the countries at war.

We have already seen that our nominal merchant navy is infinitely weaker than in 1914. In reality it is in a still worse case since far too many so-called British ships are owned by foreigners and manned by them almost exclusively. This has been one of the crying scandals of the merchant navy for some years. Foreign ships registered as British have been hovering like vultures around the Spanish carcass. Thus it is unlikely that we could rely on the whole of our merchant navy, since foreign manned and only nominally British owned ships might (unless in British waters), go elsewhere for cargoes at the outbreak of war. Moreover, conditions of pay and life in the merchant navy have reduced the number of British seamen, both in officers and men, well below the numbers needed for any expansion, or indeed, any control by officers and men over the total number of ships flying the red ensign. The number of officers in training and apprentices is appallingly low because of the poor prospects offered. It may well be that British shipping companies could not afford to do anything better for their men in view of having to compete with subsidized shipping in the hands of other great powers. But these powers, to take only Italy and the U.S.A. as examples, have looked upon a very large merchant navy as part of their Naval Policy. We who need food, oil and other supplies simply to exist have been almost alone in neglecting our merchant navy.[1] The mistress of the seas is likely to become the beggar on the waterfront.

There is one last danger to be reckoned with in our merchant navy. We are, as has been shown, desperately short of British personnel. We will be shorter still in a crisis, since nearly all the best of the officers and many of the men are in the R.N.V.R. These will be needed for the Navy proper. While, if there is trouble in India, the Lascars may or may not be depended on as crews for the merchant ships, which they man on the

[1] It is true that the tramp shipping subsidy has done something towards modernizing our Navy, but at the expense of scrapping a much larger number of ships in the last few years. The effects of further subsidy will take some years to become apparent in tonnage and personnel.

Orient trade routes. Nor will enemy powers be slow in fomenting trouble in the East. The merchant ships themselves will be required as tenders for the Navy in large numbers, as tankers for oiling in distant ports, as liners for hospital ships, troopships and auxiliary cruisers, and if there is any expeditionary force, to carry men, food and munitions and supplies. The Air Force alone will require a large merchant fleet to transport aeroplanes and ground staff. Thus a smaller and more vulnerable merchant navy will have to do increased duties with fewer officers and men, more foreign crews, and for the first time potentially disaffected Lascars.[1] It remains to examine what chances would exist in war time of keeping open our communications in view of our weakened mercantile marine, our increased population and our lessened ability to increase our home-grown food in an emergency.

Can the Navy defend this position even with the help of our Air Force? The last war is rarely the criterion in tactics for the next, but fundamental strategy is ageless. Sea power in any maritime country is the age-old key to success. But to-day we have air power which is only partly analogous to sea power, yet just as vital. We know that apart from land warfare we have three elements to consider—the surface of the sea, the air.

[1] The writer does not necessarily imply mutinous crews, but sabotage such as Capt: von Rintelen carried out with the help of the New York Irish in the last war.

above, and the waters below. The tactics may differ, but the central strategy remains the same; only for three elements instead of one. There is this difference, that air power is, to use an Irishism, amphibious, and thus is only half concerned with the sea and naval strategy. England's concern in air defence is on land and water. We have a new element primed with fresh danger which must be considered separately. Generally speaking, the chances of surprise in war have narrowed to the air. Use of the ether and the air have largely removed surprise in close combat from land and sea. But the aerial vessels have not yet removed the need for a navy. An enemy fleet, regardless of home air forces, could still destroy our shipping and our home ports if we had no navy, for anti-aircraft-fire power has grown side by side with the power of aircraft. So we could rely on air power to defend us on the sea as little as we could in 1914. But the need of defending our merchant ships from attack by air at any point within reach of enemy aircraft is a new duty for our Navy, and may mean a much more elaborate convoy system. It is as if a shepherd had been given a rifle to deal with the wolves, which attacked his flock, and was suddenly faced by eagles swooping simultaneously upon his lambs. But the shepherd is infinitely weaker than he was twenty-three years ago, and the wolves are stronger.

In 1914 we had a Navy on a two-power standard. Now we have a Navy which is theoretically.

on a one-power standard. It is relatively strong as a battle fleet, but woefully weak for guerrilla warfare attacking our shipping.

But in 1914 to 1918 there was never a maritime nation more fortunately placed for communications than ourselves. Not only had Germany very few submarines, Austria was her only naval ally for even with the *Goeben* Turkey was bottled in the Sea of Marmora. We had the navies of France, Russia, Japan, and later of Italy and the U.S.A. and all the shipping and shipbuilding capacity of the world to draw upon. The German navy, except for one Pacific squadron which was soon destroyed, was encircled in the North Sea. Yet we had at one time less than seventeen days' supply of food in the country. The *Emden*,[1] as a lone raider, required what to-day would be most of our cruiser force on the look-out for her in the Pacific. The lesson of armed raiders in the last war will not be forgotten in the next, nor will aeroplanes be of use in looking for a disguised armed raider. People who say the submarine menace has been ended by depth charges from all-seeing airmen are shutting their eyes to any new submarine technique. Submarines to-day have a very long range for cruising, and they can be just as dangerous to our food supplies in the Doldrums and the Roaring Forties as in home waters. If our

[1] The physical damage done by the *Emden* was slight; her mere presence paralysed the moneylenders of Madras and disorganized tea and hemp shipments from the Bay of Bengal.

cruisers and destroyers hunt them they can do so only by leaving the battle fleet unattended and the home waters naked to attack. To defend the trade routes in only one of the seven seas will be to leave the other six free for anyone's sport and pleasure. To-day the Pacific from Easter Island to New Zealand, and from the Antarctic to Honolulu is patrolled by two cruisers and two small sloops.

We are building a new Navy rapidly. In five years it will possess two-thirds of the relative strength in material that it possessed in 1914. But it still takes seven years to make an able seaman. No amount of 'gadgets' on a ship make up for this deficiency in men, although naval recruitment is very good.

In a few years we will have a first-class Air Force, equal to any in the world. But so have France, Germany, Italy, Russia, and the U.S.A.

The Air Force cannot defend us at a distance away from home, but, if they attempted to do so, they would use up additional transport. The Air Force cannot defend shipping in the narrow seas at night or in dirty weather. The Navy, except by a miracle of a world combined against one great power, could only defend our supplies in home waters.

Even if these forces could guarantee us safety by an incredible effort, they would be like soldiers meant for service abroad turned policemen at home. The object of Navy and Air Force is to produce decisive results in battle. By making them into glorified special constables war could neither be waged nor ended. The use of a fighting force lies in aggression, or defeating aggression against itself. The value of air attack lies in surprise. The main duty of our Air Force would be to paralyse enemy centres of manufacture and distribution of arms (to-day all industry is armament industry) or of supply. Likewise they are called on to defend by attack, or otherwise, our own vulnerable position. Hence, war comes literally like a shooting star. For it has been established that if the Port of London were paralysed England would be near starvation, even if every port were open, so specialized has distribution become and so reliant are we on imports.

Naval strategy differs only in speed and limitation of movement from air strategy. The Navy is meant to force naval decisions, not merely to hunt raiders in remote atolls.[1]

We have no choice but to decide that war to-day means famine, unless we take measures before it is too late. If we have not seen it other powers have, and the forces of disruption know it. A complacent Press (with a few honourable exceptions) and a complacent Government are 'public' blankets No. 1 and No. 2 at the cellar door in

[1] The last war might have ended soon after Jutland had we been able to force a decision then. But, because of the necessity to guard our sea communications, we did not dare to risk a decision in German waters.

which we shelter from the strong gas of reality. A good dose of it would not poison; but it would invigorate. While we are in a position to be starved in a few months, or days, we are inviting attack through those who wish to see chaos and from those who are land-hungry and look on our under-populated Empire as a heritage of which they are worthy and ourselves unworthy.

CHAPTER III

THE EFFECTS OF HUNGER

THOSE who have seen hungry mobs can skip this chapter. They know. But the vast majority of our countrymen will say, " My dear fellow, those sort of things don't happen with us; we'll always muddle through somehow, and, in any case, the Englishman's sense of humour will carry us through." It is for them that this book is written —to awaken them before it is too late to the cataclysm which looms ahead, and to show them how fear may yet unite us and so make a freer, healthier, and more happy land. Sense of humour in the face of difficulty is too often another name for laziness and dislike of doing the difficult thing. It is easier to laugh off misfortune than to overcome it. The unemployed have long known short commons, and individuals have suffered bitterly, but for 800 years this country has never known the foot of the invader and never, as a whole, had to tighten its belt. Hence, there is this pervading sense of unreality with which we face our dangers. But there will be no sense of humour on an empty belly.

To live on genuine short commons demands discipline for a nation; to live on next to nothing, working and fighting with order and self-control, demands a miracle of stamina in the masses, and a miracle of leadership in higher places. When genuine famine occurs, nothing remains but every man for himself. Had the writer no regard for the qualities of endurance and character in our people, he would not have troubled to write this book, but have sought a happier and safer corner of the earth in which to start afresh. There is no need to minimize our finer qualities when we face the results of famine. It is because of these qualities that Britain is worth saving. And so we must face reality.

The first effect of war will be the hoarding of supplies by a favoured minority. The second will be a rapid dislocation of supplies. Certain ports will be temporarily or permanently closed through enemy actions; certain convoys will not reach their destination, or parts of convoys will be sunk before they even reach the points of assembly, which in the last war were generally near the Azores.

All this will strain the system of distribution based on peace-time organization to the utmost as ordinary supplies in hand at the outbreak of war become used up. Military needs of transport and demand for oil will make most inland road transport a mere skeleton service. This will mean that serious undernourishment, and, perhaps, food rioting will occur in some places, while other parts of England will be living in plenty. Industrial workers and farm labourers, who have not been

41

called to the Colours, will have to work very long hours, and so will require more healthy food than they do now.[1] Undernourishment and disaffection will go hand in hand after the first flare of propaganda for war has died down. Little by little food ships will not arrive, and neutrals will no longer take the risk for their shipping. The areas of shortage[2] will grow like mushrooms, and panic will appear. Probably air raids will have already made the meaning of panic plain. Morale may rapidly be sapped, and England will be as ripe for revolution as Petrograd in 1917. This picture of the advent of famine will only happen slowly if we have a very strong Air Force to prevent the bombing of London and east coast ports. It will come slowly only if we are lucky enough to start the war with very strong naval allies, which can guarantee large parts of our trade routes or release most of the Navy from service in home waters.

Let us consider famine in England in whatever form it comes. First of all, in every great city there is a scum of subhuman population willing to take any chance of a breakdown in law and order. Such have neither respect for property or persons. They are the willing tools of the com-

[1] See " Report on Food Conditions in Germany " (Cmd. 280) 1919.

[2] Students of the question of supply in the last war will see this point at once, since mere over-congestion at the port of departure or the port of reception is often more serious than an actual shortage of food.

munist, since revolution means an opportunity to
gratify their lusts. Some of these are naturally the
dregs of English blood. But many are alien.
Foreign invasion of England has not happened in
war time. It has happened in the last hundred years
of peace. Anyone who has been able to notice with
his own eyes the foreign invasion of London should
read Colonel Lane's *The Alien Menace* to see the
extent to which it has been carried on. Half the
European conspiracies of the Left in the last fifty
years have been hatched in London. These immi-
grants have invaded the slums and the high places
as well. It should not be forgotten that those
aliens who now appear to have a stake in this
country have a stake also in many others. But
most of those, who are obscure, have a definite
stake in revolution and no instinct for or interest
in English life and tradition. One by one they
have 'muscled in' on the Englishman's livelihood till they are everywhere in key positions.
With them has come corruption and disrespect for
the ancient decencies; at the same time we are
seething with misplaced but genuine idealism.
Misplaced idealism has always been the evangelist
of the most bestial revolutions. The communist
is trained to take advantage of the Kerensky
periods of oratory, indecision, and conflicting
loyalties.

This, then, is the spawning-ground for panic,
looting, revolution, and wholesale bloodshed.
Among these would be the paid, trained, and

disciplined communist giving some order and direction to the looting and riots. Key functions like light, water supply, and drains in a big city are easy to disorganize and thus intensify panic and spread epidemic disease.

After the towns had been looted a swarm of starving, diseased, and desperate population would spread itself over the surrounding countryside, glad of grass and dead rats to eat, killing and devouring, like locusts, any living thing in its path. Unless by a miracle such a thing were localized there soon would be no more left of England's manhood than there was after the Black Death.

If men consider this picture fantastic and far-fetched, then they have not learnt, or will not learn, from the lessons of past and contemporary history. And it should be added that not only war, or civil war, but the failure of the European or American financial system might make famine a reality among us. We have only to cast our minds back to the relatively minor financial crisis of 1931 to remember the desperate efforts to save the pound, and to recollect Mr. MacDonald electioneering with million-mark notes worth a few pence. French finance is not yet out of the wood, and much of our world-wide frozen credit is frozen waste paper. A breakdown of government in the United States would be almost certain to cause disaster here. Some acute observers—American, European, and Asiatic—consider that in the next three years this is possible. It might not last long, but long enough to upset the world's financial system.

If, as the writer believes, it must be the case that the risk of war implies the equal risk of starvation at home, then the question must arise as to why we are proposing to spend a minimum of £1,500,000,000 on rearmament without so far making any provision to feed ourselves. Nobody but an infant in arms could suppose (if he has any true knowledge of the situation) that the present proposals for British agriculture would even touch the problem. It may be argued quite rightly that to have magnificent fighting equipment will act as a deterrent to our possible enemies. Up to this point few realists will dispute the wisdom of strong forces. But our enemies are not slow to realize that all the ships, guns, and aeroplanes which we can produce will be unavailing if we have not sufficient trained men to man them; and that, above all, they will be useless if we cannot feed our forces or our people.

Surely it is high time the 'plain man' understood the position and took a hand to prevent what must happen in a crisis, and the slow poison of our people now going on in peace. It is time that he understood that an armament policy without the inconvenience of an agricultural effort suits the politicians, for it creates a boom without dear food propaganda and so makes the unemployment figures satisfactory. It suits the international financiers, since it creates new loans without making us self-supporting. It suits the professional pacifists, since it gives us a force with which they can clamour to intervene always on the side of revolution, for without food at home we rely on " collective security ", which is the collective insecurity of world depression.

PART II
Iron Rations

... A Harpy has flown over our feast.
NIETZSCHE.

INTRODUCTION

WE have seen that there is an undeniable danger of war. We have seen that if there is war, then the danger from famine and the panic and revolution which famine would cause are so terrible that nothing might be left of our sound stocks. One thing is certain, we will not this time have a war which could give us command of sea as we had it in 1914. In future we will need command of the atmosphere as well.

But throughout this analysis of our dangers there has appeared one recurrent fact. A healthy agriculture in Britain would, with strong fighting forces, save us from fear of attack, but without a healthy agriculture we must have a heel of Achilles for everyone to see as an invitation to attack. A healthy agriculture would mean healthier bodies and, therefore, healthier minds. A healthy agriculture would break the unemployment problem, and by doing all these things would give us back stability and hope, self-respect and independence. The answer of the soil comes in the long cycle of farming practice. If we know the soil is a master worth serving, then we must make provision to serve and not exploit it for immediate needs. So our method must be twofold. First we must create a shield of food reserves, then behind this, with necessary patience, we can labour to become self-sufficient.

CHAPTER IV
THE NEED FOR FOOD
RESERVES

W HEN war is over the sword is sold for junk;
but the plough is pawned for bankers'
dividends. Yet when war is imminent even the
newly tempered British sword is useless unless
the soil be ready for the share. These sentences
epitomize the last two decades of our history.

The soil is not ready for the share. Since 1918
some £3,000,000 a year have been taken from the
land in death duties, most of which has not been
replaced. From 1915 to 1922 the land was short
of every kind of labour and of livestock. Yet the
land was in that same period forced to produce
from its reserves of fertility at a very high rate.
In that way, too, the land lost capital which has
never been replaced. For when the repeal of the
Corn Production Act betrayed our farmers in
1922, they were told that they must farm economically. In other words, they had to compete
with the new world exploiting virgin land, and
with the old world subsidizing their only export
market, namely Great Britain. Thus our farmers,
to keep alive, had to exploit their land already
exploited to save England in war time. So land

has not only suffered by the decay of farm buildings, the neglect of fences and ditches and drains,
it has also suffered from economically enforced bad
farming. Many an old and wiser worker on the
land can recall when such and such a rough grazing grew a good crop of oats, or where scrannel
crops are failing amidst docks and thistles on a
field under plough, how it grew twelve sacks of
wheat when " I wur working for y'ure grandad."

Recently it was stated in the House of Lords
that through the aid of the new Marketing Board
plans could be made for a rapid expansion of agricultural production in war time. Never was greater
moonshine radiated over an urban population. The
soil is not a factory that can work three eight-hour
shifts in the day at peak production. It is a living
thing that will only respond to the way in which
it is served.

Joseph saved Egypt by " cornering " the surplus grain of seven good years against seven lean
years. For the soil itself one must reverse the
procedure and give back before you can take out
from it.

Thus to-day it is far less possible to feed these
islands from our own soil than it was twenty-three
years ago when we had had fifteen years of good
farming to draw on for reserves of fertility. Generally speaking, in our fields at present there are no
reserves. Artificial manures which could have a
great temporary effect (whatever the consequences
of their use) on fertile land cannot justly help

the situation when the land has been robbed of its humus as it has been to-day. The whole aspect of soil fertility will be dealt with in a later chapter. But what concerns us now is that no hope of serious expansion in war time can take place until we have set about reviving soil fertility. It will take three seasons before we can see noticeable results from this revival. We can, however, by beginning with the policy which will give fertility, increase our livestock production almost immediately with pigs, arable sheep and cattle, and possibly poultry. This will involve for some years a substantial but temporary increase in import of foodstuffs for livestock. If we do not increase our livestock production we will never restore the fertility of our land.

Many European countries which farm for export have already become mere processors of the raw material for livestock production. These have arrived at a policy of selling off the land large quantities of products in butter, sugar, bacon, cheese, wheat, and malting barley, etc. To do this enormous quantities of milling offals, maize, and cotton cakes, etc., have had to be imported. We in England have done this as much as any other country, although Denmark is the classic example of a country turned into a butter and bacon factory using the raw products of the new world. The acreage under sugar-beet is now about 350,000, and that under potatoes is about 600,000. A considerable part of this acreage seventy years ago

53

would have been devoted to animal fodder crops, so that when we talk of our agricultural production off the land being so much, upon which we can rely for food in a crisis, we deceive ourselves, unless we remember the debit side of the bill which is for animal feeding stuffs bought from abroad. It is as if a country which could only produce iron and steel and had no fuel, oil, coal, or water-power, relied for its munitions in war time on its peace-time figures of steel production, and neglected to have reserves of fuel. It would either be stupidity or dishonest book-keeping, or both.

Thus unless we are going to issue a dishonest prospectus for war-time risks, we must have a human and animal food reserve in this country as well as £1,500,000,000 worth of armaments. At present we have issued a dishonest prospectus to the people. It may be that the Cabinet are simply 'guinea-pig' directors suffering from ignorance and stupidity, but the fact remains that we have no food reserves, and the public utterance of responsible politicians would imply neither need for large reserves nor intention to form them.

What are the arguments against a food reserve? Let us take the need for one year of reserves in human food and animal food as our requirement. If we increase our livestock and livestock food reserves, our only other vital reserves need be wheat for human beings. Butter and condensed milk would be valuable but not vital, nor would sugar be necessary. If we had food reserves for animals, we would be wise not to have them in cotton-cake and oil cakes available only for animal use, but in extra wheat, barley, maize, and oats, which could be used for human food as well. The 1928 Report of the Ministry of Agriculture on the marketing of wheat in England and Wales said that there was enough storage-room for nearly one year's supply of wheat. At that time this space was being turned to other uses, and to-day we could not rely on anything like that amount of space, even if it were politic. It is not politic to do so, as the less wheat we store in reserve at the great ports the better. Therefore, it would entail building inland silos for wheat. In fact, it would be wise to restore the old inland miller to his rightful position where he served his neighbourhood. This would entail considerable expense, about the same amount as we now spend in building new schools for children, who will in ten years not be there to fill them. Thus expense of storage is the first argument against reserves.

It will mean that some national agency will have to go into the world's grain market to buy the available stores. This also may be expensive, as wheat prices have shot up. Battleships are likewise more expensive now, and cannot be eaten when they have served their turn as wheat reserves can be. But it might also mean a measure of nationalization for one of the great importing interests. This is the second argument. Yet in spite of the obvious disadvantages, nationalization of international middlemen interests might be as healthy as nationalization of individual production is unhealthy. From 1923 to 1932 Canada exported more than the 240,000,000 bushels of wheat annually required to feed this country. Now Canada has, on the average, for many years been forced to keep a wheat reserve larger than our annual needs at home simply in order not to have to destroy her wheat harvests in years when there were not enough buyers. Thus, put plainly, we should merely do for national safety what Canada has done for economic reasons. The storing of grain for food reserves is not the continuous purchase of stuffs which perish or become obsolete and therefore necessitate a fresh purchase each year. The national debt would not go up after the initial purchase and erection of storage facilities. The grain would be consumed and replaced *pari passu*.

The vast majority of national debt is pure liability, money for shells, guns and ships, Government buildings, schools, roads, etc. But a year's reserve of grain is a reality and is an edible asset.

We would need, therefore, some 240,000,000 bushels or 30,000,000 quarters of wheat for human food reserves and some five million[1] tons of maize,

---

[1] This figure is arrived at by allowing a fair ration of imported food for all our stock of pigs, cattle and poultry and allowing for our own home-grown barley, oats, and beans and peas to take care of the increase in livestock advocated later in this book.

barley, and oats for animal feeding stuffs. The total cost of this would be about £100,000,000 to £110,000,000, plus the cost of storage. If we can afford £542 per bed for new lunatic asylums, those who are still sane should be able to see that grain reservoirs are a sounder investment in bricks and mortar.

The last argument against grain reserves is that our moist climate makes the storage of grain risky in face of damp and mildew. Grain reserves have been stored in England and Europe from time immemorial. Grain ships under sail carry wheat from Australia on the exceedingly wet ocean. It takes them something like six months to arrive. But their wheat is consumed nevertheless, and often in England. Under modern air-conditioning there is no argument or even excuse for grain not keeping.

Thus the arguments against a wheat reserve are no more than those of expediency. They sum up as being costly, as being difficult, as being possibly upsetting to international trade, and as being possibly unnecessary. The last argument can only weigh with those who consider that the next war will be exactly like the last, which is nonsense.

But the importers' reasons against a reserve are plausible. A wheat reserve to be worth anything in war time must be placed inland; independent local millers might start up again, or the tiny few that remain might again become important. The whole scheme of squashing any competition by the small man would receive a set-back. Concentration and not devolution is what the importers want. If they had not wanted centralization, they would not have applied the " inexorable pressure of economic tendencies " in the last few years to the country miller.

There is another advantage in reserves. Speculation in wheat would receive a nasty shock. Speculation is always at the producers' expense, and generally at the consumers', but with the wheat reserves in Britain rather than abroad less speculation is possible. In 1935 the wheat harvest in England was being carted in such ideal weather that it was possible for nearly a fortnight to thresh grain direct from the field. Now English farmers have always been told that their own production was so infinitesimal that it could never affect world prices. Yet for that brief fortnight, when having threshed their wheat they had to get rid of it, English milling wheat only fetched eighteen shillings a quarter. Then came the rain and wheat had to be stored in rick for threshing in the winter. Wheat in England suddenly went up to about twenty-eight shillings a quarter, an immediate rise of about 50 per cent. when the farmer was no longer forced to sell the wheat which he could not store. World conditions had remained unaltered. Such manipulation as this could not happen in the future, if we stored our own wheat reserve.

We have an exchange equalization fund. This so far has gambled successfully in keeping exchanges stable which, in other and not less real circumstances, might crash. This reacts for finance so that money markets the world over may be steady. No one sees in this anything but a wise precaution for the stability of world trade and the propping up of otherwise unstable foreign politics. Yet, if we bought wheat to hold for our own grain reserves it would act as an international price stabilizer of a world commodity. Obviously, it would be to our advantage if there was a surplus in any country, especially a Dominion, to over-buy on such occasions, and similarly within the margin of safety, to withhold purchase temporarily when there were world shortages. Since no one has con- sidered it costly and impracticable to erect grain elevators for storage against a possible surplus in the producing country, one can only suppose that this is a means of depressing world prices by a carry-over of the previous season and so ensuring a glut in the following year.

That we suffer from a financial veto (regardless of democracy) in this matter seems clear when we consider the gold reserve. Orthodox financiers for some reason or other do not think it funny to have anything from two to five hundred million pounds worth of bar gold in the Bank of England vaults. It is not used for commercial purposes, but simply to satisfy the financial system that by keeping gold without real uses we make the financial system of paper real. It might as well have stayed in the ground unmined for all the good it does us. But if we exchanged some of this gold for edible assets, such as a food reserve, it is considered bad business. Veal is welcome to the starving belly, but the garnished golden calf would make cold comfort. Not many years ago Earl Baldwin virtually told a Conservative conference at Birmingham that one could not have armaments and credit in the City of London. Yet to-day we have found armaments necessary because national credit must demand national strength; in the same way we will discover that food reserves are part of national strength and therefore of credit. The national arguments for a food reserve are overwhelming. In war time our Navy and Air Force would be freed of anxiety over the food position to attack our enemies when and where they were most vulnerable. No one can estimate what such a freedom of action established by a food reserve at home might have done to lessen the length of the last war, and so have saved in life and treasure and morale. In war time also the very knowledge that we have well distributed food reserves will keep up our morale, and save us from the inevitable dangers which the threat of famine would bring.

In the second place, it would free our foreign policies to act in the best way for Great Britain. There is a tale, presumably apochryphal, told of a meeting among the leading representatives of the Powers in a recent crisis involving Europe. The Englishman, fresh from a spectacular dash in sleeping-cars across Europe, was taking a 'strong stand'. Whereupon he was reminded in a 'frank and friendly' statement that our Air Force was fifth among the great Powers and our Navy was small and partly obsolete and that we had no expeditionary force or food reserves, so that his 'strong stand' had no backing. The meeting then broke up and our representative took the first train *de luxe* (somewhat less spectacularly) back to England to consult his colleagues at home. Whether Earl Baldwin's lips became sealed at that moment or later on, history does not relate. But although apochryphal, the story is real in the sense of illustrating the pitiful weakness and vacillation of our foreign policy in the post-war years. Our bluff can always be called so long as we are vulnerable.

If it is the case that we could be forced into panic by air raids and quickly starved in the event of war, other nations know this, and so even in peace time we will be unable to speak with authority among the nations of Europe. With a strong Air Force and Navy plus a food reserve, even with a less well-disciplined people than we should have, no nation or nations would dare carry their diplomacy to the point of risking war, for they would be hard put to it to force a quick decision, whereas we would have everything in our favour. Thus until we have this food reserve we will not be independent.

Likewise, if the present financial system were to

crash under the heavy superstructure of its own debt, our position in England would be extremely unhealthy.

Mussolini is reported to have said that no country can hope to put through a policy of internal regeneration, unless it can make its banking system serve national before international interests. Unless we have a sufficient food reserve at home, it will be impossible to tackle our worst evils. The threat of starvation is one no statesman can answer, if it is a real threat. If we could survive for a year on our own fat, we should have won the first round against the internationalist in the battle for national health. Germany could not have attempted the task of building up national health and national independence unless she had been able to produce nearly 80 per cent. of her agricultural requirements. Italy could never have survived the Abyssinian crisis if she had not been very nearly self-sufficient.

The good effect of tariffs on our home production wherever they have been applied has been obvious, and yet our protective policy has never really touched agriculture, and has only been very tentatively applied to many other things as the figures for manufactured imports show. The history of the Ottawa Conference, the world conference of 1932, and all our subsequent trade pacts, make it clear that finance and foreign trade has had consideration over everything else. Thus our policy has never been truly national. Russia can get as much money as she needs under the Export Credit Facilities Act, but there is no such benefit to British agriculture as there has been to collective farming on the Steppes.

It is plain that food reserve is vital in war time. It is also by the same token vital to us in any home policy which has as its purpose national health and independence. It is indeed the first step in making it possible to restore some measure of national health by a regenerate agriculture.

The voice of the party follower in this matter is too often an echo of the average financial mind. The argument is roughly as follows: "Yes, I agree, a wheat reserve would have been a good thing, but, my dear fellow, you are too late. A couple of years ago we could have bought all we needed, but at the present price of wheat it's out of the question." And at this point a look of relief at having a good excuse for avoiding an awkward problem comes into his face. But the fact remains that the present price of wheat is one, which for the first time for some years, has paid the farmer to grow wheat. It is not more than it was a few years ago, and no more than it should be in a world where the farmer receives a just price for his efforts. It would cost between £60,000,000 and £70,000,000 instead of £48,000,000 two years ago. The cost of aeroplanes and battleships has advanced enormously also, but that does not seem to strike the politician.

If there is likely to be a comparative world

shortage of wheat to-day instead of a large carry-over, it is more urgent than ever to have a wheat reserve. Not only would wheat in war time be more expensive to buy, it would be more difficult to come by, and every wheat ship sunk would make the home position more dangerous if there were not enough wheat to go round. So the importance of a wheat reserve at home is emphasized and not diminished by the present high prices and relative shortage. An argument against a food reserve on the grounds of cost is analogous to a rich Polar explorer setting out with one quarter of his estimated necessary ration of pemmican, because there is a rising market on which to buy it, while he compensates for this by a larger number of sleighs than he has dogs to draw and an extra quantity of medical supplies against tropical diseases.

The policy should be one year's supply. Our own food reserves in England from home-grown wheat is enough for about six weeks; our average day-to-day reserve of imported wheat is enough for about another six weeks, if we are lucky. But the home-grown food reserve is available only, and then in part, for the months from October to March, by which the last of it will probably be threshed. The majority of it will have been threshed by January. So that at any given time we require enough wheat to carry on until the next harvest. But if war should come in the spring, we would require not only enough to last till the next harvest is gathered, but enough with careful management to last until the following season's cropping can be put on an emergency basis to grow a much larger quantity of wheat, for this crop has to be planned twelve months ahead to make sure of good results. Even should the next war prove to be a long one, we should have, with a year's food reserve, almost eighteen months free of anxiety, in which case we would probably have managed to bring in enough stores to carry on for another six months if our own agriculture in the meantime has been accelerated. We would, by using the plough mercilessly for continuous cropping, probably be able to produce treble our present output of wheat and barley in the South and of oats in the North, and perhaps double our potato output. This, if we started with sufficient livestock, would enable us to survive at least three and probably four years of warfare, as far as food supplies are concerned.

But it would be essential to have at the same time enough feeding-stuffs to use for our livestock for at least a year, after which we could slaughter breeding stock for extra rations and so save, to some extent, in cereal for human consumption, as well as in rations for animals.

Finally, it will be necessary to have our food stores inland and as widely distributed as possible. The military reasons for this are obvious. The farmer, who stores all his grain or hay for convenience in one rick-yard or barn, risks losing the

E
65

whole by an outbreak of fire, while if he builds ricks scattered over the fields, his risks are diminished in proportion to the number of ricks he has separately placed. But the risk is diminished even more, because in the fields his grain is not stored near any inflammable fuel or other causes of fire. So it is not only that risk from air raids are spread by scattered inland stores, but they are out of the way of the immediate military objectives.

Then there is a civil consideration. A disorganized or skeleton transport could distribute from many centres much more easily than from one or two if railways or bridges were blown up. Thus the danger and panic of famine would be minimized.

The final consideration is one which dovetails into a long-range farming policy. If local mills, drying plants and silos were available to the number of two or three or more in every county, it would make it far easier for the farmer to thresh and store his grain in ideal conditions than now, and also to mill the feeding-stuffs for his animals that he grew on his own farm. The wise farmer will prefer to feed the grain grown on his own healthy land to grain grown on land the health of which he is ignorant. Much animal disease comes from feeding the products of unhealthy soil. The farmer who has to sell wheat or barley as a cash crop will also have the advantage that he can store his grain properly and sell it, when there is not a local glut on the market caused, as we saw in some

66

cases, by fine harvest weather when everyone is threshing grain at once out of the field. This consideration is particularly important in the case of malting barley. Though he does not do this universally the brewer can force down prices in the autumn—when it is generally necessary to thresh —so that the farmer must take any price, or feed his malting barley to the pigs.

This makes the storage facilities inland of economic as well as of military value, just as storage facilities plus a grain reserve is of economic value in the long run to stabilize fluctuating prices in the world market.

There is another economic advantage in food storage. It would prevent the importation of white, flour into this country. Our own mills would perform this work, and the milling offals would be available for feeding stock in this country. If inland milling again became the rule, we would not have the spectacle of bran and middlings being exported to Denmark by ship at a cheaper price than our own farmers can buy them at home.

The arguments for a year's supply of animal feeding-stuffs are the same as those for a year's supply of human foodstuffs. They would enable us to keep our animals more or less intact for a year, while our farming system was placed on an emergency basis for the maximum production of cereal crops for sale off the farm. These reserves should consist largely of cereals which can be used for human or animal consumption, and so spread

67

our risks as widely as possible. Some oil-cakes would probably be necessary as a sop to the present system, in which they are part of our own industrial by-products.

The cost of the erection of the food stores and reconditioning of existing ones cannot be estimated, as there are no comparable English figures in existence. But if we hold that £1,500,000,000 is a minimum figure with which we will be faced for rearmament, then the absolutely necessary cost of food stores, which will not become out of date like battleships and aeroplanes, is relatively unimportant.

PART III

Slow Poison

And some are great in rank and wealth and power,
  And some renowned for genius and for worth:
And some are poor and mean, who brood and cower
  And shrink from notice, and accept all dearth
Of body, heart and soul, and leave to others
All boons of life; yet these and those are brothers,
  The saddest and the weariest men on earth.

JAMES THOMPSON
The City of Dreadful Night

INTRODUCTION

THE necessity of using our own land against starvation has become apparent, even though we take emergency measures such as food reserves against a shortage in war time. New deserts are being made and the acres of good soil are narrowing. The chapter on world erosion will show that world conditions will sometime, even if they do not at present, make us return for the necessities of life to our own soil in peace as well as war. But if we analyse the declining health of our own people it makes the arguments overwhelming for tilling our own soil well and wisely. It is necessary to realize that there is another form of starvation, which is going on unseen before our eyes. Because it is less spectacular it is often taken for granted, yet because it is the more subtle it is the more dangerous. This is the moral starvation and the slow physical starvation proceeding now throughout this island. If we are to have a low morale and poor physique in the fullest sense of the word, neither arms nor fuel and food reserves will avail us. Nutrition is synonymous with existence. It is in the air we breathe, the sun that shines on us, the water that we drink as well as the food we eat.

71

Because nutrition is synonymous with existence it is the foundation of sanity and morale and the only medium in which it will be possible to regenerate the failing stock of sound types which once made England the world's leader.

CHAPTER V

ANALYSIS OF THE SUBNORMAL

IN his book, *Towards Armageddon*, General Fuller has stressed to the full our need for national discipline, and has touched on the importance of home agriculture, as well as food reserves. At this time there need be no excuse for reiterating his plea in different words and in a parallel context. In the case of air raids alone, if any order is to be preserved, discipline is absolutely essential. It is doubly necessary when short rations or a breakdown of food supplies occur. For it must always be more necessary when the best of our manhood will be needed for active warfare, and when, moreover, long and sustained effort on the land and in the workshop is demanded. By this the writer does not mean the apathetic indifference of the slave, which submits to any crack of the whip; he means the spiritual discipline to a purpose which reacts nobly to sacrifice necessary for that purpose. It is far easier to obtain this spiritual discipline in healthy bodies. And bodies are not sound unless they are properly nourished. Brilliant and perverted brains often go with unsound bodies, but you cannot hope to get sane and balanced reactions without real health. Yet because we have lost touch with the soil we have lost this consideration for a regenerate nation.

The true reactions to discipline and self-respect we are deemed by our rulers to have lost. Compulsory Insurance Acts, often protecting the thriftless at the expense of the thrifty, and above all the compulsory education laws, are all part of a system which tells men and women that in things wherein they should judge for themselves and show responsibility they are not fit, while they are cajoled into believing they have freedom, if they can agitate in Hyde Park or vote on matters of which they must be utterly ignorant, such as the future of India or Japanese policy in Manchukuo. The politicians dare not ask us to do national work instead of receiving the dole, to ask our women to learn the forgotten arts of housecraft, to ask our men to accept conscription for defence, or the boys to perform disciplined manual labour for the common weal in the labour camp. That is called unthinkable compulsion.

Yet they are wrong. In the working men lies the aristocratic instinct and the desire for responsible craftsmanship and family life. In spite of everything that has been done by industrialism and the State they are waiting to be led to salvation, and out of the slough of self-disrespect into which they have been driven. The fine stuff of English life is still there. The cataclysm of famine and revolution would not matter if there was nothing to save, but it is because these working men and the good men surviving in every class are liable to be wiped out, that we must first of all consider physical health and the way of re-generation through a healthy agriculture. This brings us to the physical starvation of our people which, as nutrition is synonymous with existence, goes far to explain the spiritual starvation and the lack of real discipline from which we are suffering. It is far easier to get spiritual discipline from a healthy body than a botched and maimed body. The body is older than the mind in our inheritance, and, therefore, while the mind often does react on the body, it is the body which reacts always on the mind.

The rejections of recruits for the last war have shown that even then we were on the average a " C 3 " nation. Far from doing anything to right it, the process has since gone on. Housing, it is true, has had some good effects at enormous cost, but it has still to be faced as a problem animated by national purpose rather than statistics for vote-catching. In other ways the position has gone from bad to worse.[1]

Many earnest workers who have striven for health will have a shock of surprise to read this.

[1] Dr. Howard Mummery, Chairman of the Association of Industrial Medical Officers, revealed the other day that workers insured under the N.H.I. Act lose on an average 28 days' work a year through illness compared with 16.5 days fifteen years ago. ("Some Facts for Employers"—National Milk Publicity Council.)

None the less, the facts speak for themselves. From
1930 onwards an average of nearly 2,000,000 men
and women with their families have been existing
on the dole and poor relief. That in itself means
the physical and mental depression of one-fifth of
our people. But the industrial revolution, and
later modern education and the twentieth-century
fashion of feminism, which despises any virtue
which has to do with good housekeeping, has
meant that the knowledge of how to use even the
dole has disappeared. Bully-beef occasionally,
white bread, sugar and tea without fresh milk have
been the usual food; green vegetables in the worst
of the depressed areas are almost unknown. Thus
the effect of living on the dole has been twice as
bad as it would have been in the days when women
baked wholemeal bread and did not confine their
cooking to the use of a tin-opener. The evil of
unemployment has been with us in an aggravated
form since 1922 and, therefore, it is safe to say that
at least 15 per cent. of our people for fifteen
years have been alive on a sub-existence. This
sub-existence has been going on side by side with
a progressive degeneration of the land, from which
very many of them could have gained a living, if
we had husbanded our resources instead of our
foreign loans. Anyone, who knows the North and
the industrial areas where the clouds of unemployment are settled, knows likewise that speaking
generally, it has settled on the sturdiest of towns-
folk and not the worst. Without hope there is no

incentive to make the best of a bad job, and so the mental rot is not only started by the physical rot but nurtured by despair; it is a despair that comes entirely from the lack of leadership to give it hope.

There is another side to the question which has come from the worship of disease. We have constantly congratulated ourselves on a declining infant mortality. In fact, as Lord Dawson of Penn has pointed out, we have thereby kept alive children who would normally have died and who, from their youth to their old age, are, and will be, a constant tax on the fit. Is the steady rate of maternal mortality anything to do with this? May it not be that many women have been kept alive who are not fit to be mothers, and many fit mothers have indirectly been taxed and depressed to provide for the unfit, while the necessity to work in factories has postponed marriage until long after the best period for childbearing in a woman's life?

The birth-rate is declining steadily, and yet, in spite of such medical care as was not dreamed of fifty years ago, ante-natal clinics and modern midwifery, the maternal mortality is such that the normal function of childbirth is now widely looked upon as a sort of dread disease. This morbid attitude to childbirth surely is the acid test of national unfitness.

But the signs of morbidity are almost universal, so much so that we are apt to look upon the average as normal. People think it is quite normal

77

to have 'flu every winter, to have incessant colds, to have false teeth and to wear spectacles. Again and again one hears men—and especially women— talking with eager exhibitionism and not shame of their pathological symptoms. Many acres of good ground between Regent's Park and Wigmore Street are devoted to the ministers of these richer subjects of colitis, sinusitis, and innumerable neuroses. But it is the same among the poor. Constipation, headaches, catarrh, low spirits, gastric ulcers, and an infinite number of minor ailments are looked upon as the everyday lot of man. Even *The Times* congratulated the nation some years ago on the increased care it was receiving as evinced by the enormous increase in free medicine, as if more pills could mean anything but more poorliness.

This is borne out by the School Medical Officers' Reports, wherein really bad teeth are the lot of over two-thirds of the school children examined. It could easily be proved that 90 per cent. of the children suffer from some defect or other that is more or less a serious handicap. These may vary from rickets and spinal curvature to dental caries, chronic catarrh and flat feet. But one and all are signs of wrong nutrition or disgenic parenthood. It is likewise a sign of wrong values in this question of nutrition that we place first the endowment of disease, that is the enormous increase in hospital accommodation, research on virus and injections, together with the emphasis on surgery.

78

We should place first the way of living to prevent these things being necessary. Cases of gastric ulcer and appendicitis have been found by Sir Robert McCarrison to be almost unknown among some properly nourished hill tribes of India. Thus, important as physical training may be, it is simply asking the horse to push the cart by beginning to treat our malaise with training-grounds and gymnasia unless we cure our bad habits in eating, nay, in living, first.

Until we are able to differentiate between the average and the normal, it is vain to hope for a regeneration that is enduring. We must have a new standard in life that will make for a new standard, or an old one, in duty to, and faith in the soundest of our stocks. This is not to say that physical training for the townsman is to be rejected out of hand, but that good can best come from it, as Lord Dawson of Penn has said, by paying attention to its potential leaders (the best of our types), who may inspire by the example of their living. What we have done is to take the most obvious side of the German system, and to apologize for it by laying emphasis on our non-military intentions, while we have neglected the deeper issues which make Germany an example we have had to follow whether we like it or not.

It is the labour camps which have put into practice the intense desire to serve Germany as individuals and citizens of all classes working as one whole. And among women the labour camps are primarily their enthusiastic response to learning their job as housewives and guardians of health.[1]

It is average to have bad teeth at twelve; it is normal to have sound teeth at forty; it is average to be constipated, but it is normal to evacuate food wastes twelve hours and not thirty-six hours after eating. It is normal but not average to have strong sight and straight bodies. It is normal but not average for women to be able to select and cook good food. So one could go on, paragraph by paragraph. But until we get the standard of looking to the normal as each man's personal duty to achieve, for himself, we shall be decadent.

The present results are evident from the figures of rejection on physical grounds of recruits for the Forces. These standards have been seriously lowered as the shortage of recruits has increased. It may be assumed that the average man who offers himself for service is not the worst physical type in the nation. He is probably the average physique in the nation. Yet 47 per cent. of these in 1935 were rejected. In Germany 78 per cent. are passed fully fit on a national conscription basis. Our own figure is worse still when we remember that about 25 per cent. of those offering themselves are so obviously unfit as not even to come up for a medical examination, and these rejections thus go

[1] See Miss Fairholme's admirable article in the July issue of the *English Review*, 1937; and see General Fuller's *Towards Armageddon*, p. 112.

unrecorded. But one striking fact has been produced by the Army's latest effort to make bricks without straw. By taking men who were found to be below standard yet not hopeless, they have, in a few months, raised many of them up to Army standard if not to normal standards. This has been done on Army rations plus discipline, plus physical training. Army rations are not ideal in regard to freshness, but they provide—compared with what most people eat—sound food in adequate quantities. Discipline and purpose has provided a mental outlook in which food could be turned to proper use. Physical training—although Army drill is doubtful in its scientific effect on the body—has, given the food and the discipline, straightened and strengthened otherwise ineffective bodies. And so we return to the outstanding question of nutrition.

Nutrition begins with the soil, but in so far as a town population is concerned, it is the housewife who is the important secondary agent of nutrition. The education of the housewife is as important to make war-time rations do fuller work, as it is to make certain of health in peace. Modern education has deprived women of their instinctive and traditional skill, by glorifying the mere acquisition of book-knowledge on subjects often unrelated to life. Secondly, modern industry has often taken her out of the home and taught her that housekeeping is only secondary to the earning of a living by herself in case her husband loses his work. The cooking arrangements of modern housing in towns have made the tin-opener far more useful than the oven. All the trend of advertisement has continually told her to save trouble in order to line the pockets of food processors. Such education in housekeeping as she has had has been to stress calories or vitamins and germs rather than to tell her what foods could make up a balanced, wholesome diet, which would banish constipation, bad teeth, soft bones, and all the troubles which spring from them. Therefore it is small blame to her to-day if she is both incapable of choosing (among rich and poor alike), the wholesome food and of cooking it properly, when she has chosen it.

It is easy to quote cases of vigorous persons who as pioneers have thriven on tinned food, coffee, and salt meat. But these were not brought up on such a diet any more than their children were, when they had settled. The pioneers generally had all the other aids to nutrition we lack : untreated water, endless fresh air and sunlight, and hard work on creative jobs. Sunlight in industrial areas is very scarce. Even on a sunny day the pall of smoke obscures the best of it. In order to make water safe for the large towns it is faintly chlorinated, which cannot be good for the people who drink it. Some fresh-cut flowers, which live in pure water, cannot survive even for a few hours in London water. The results on our bodies are slower than on cut flowers, but they are none the less sure. Such vegetables and fruit as the poor do get are very often stale, and we have no guarantee of the health of the soil on which they were grown. Anyone working near a gas-works knows how polluted may be the air which he breathes. A London fog is evidence enough of miasmic conditions from industry and crowded houses. London trees and flowers have a hard battle. But it is not only the smoke of chimneys and the gases from certain factories that pollute. A crowded street of London traffic where there is no breeze will be to the countryman almost unbearable from the highly poisonous petrol fumes.[1] To shut yourself in a garage and turn on the engine of a car is one of the most efficient ways of committing suicide. Add to this pollution the facts that the air itself is overcrowded with human beings, and that nearly everyone of them is living in a state of noise, hurry, stress, and crowded journeys to and from work, then one has the very worst conditions in which to create a healthy people. In such circumstances it is hard enough to digest good food, and next to impossible to digest bad food. No palliatives can be found to save us from the effect of bad food and bad cooking. So it is clear that morbidity, restlessness, and malaise (physical and spiritual) are our daily lot, unless we turn to healthy food, for everything else is against us.

[1] See Report on an investigation into the sickness experience of London Transport workers with special reference to digestive disturbances, by A. Bradford Hill, H.M. Stationery Office.

83

Bad food not only makes bad bodies, it makes wrong minds. The really healthy peoples are the happy peoples. These also have a sane respect for all the permanent things of life among them. There is a family feeling and a racial feeling, and a determination to guard their culture. Thus the words kind and gentle have the same meaning and derivation from kinship or within the tribe. For, we once discriminated and kept our kindness or our gentleness to foster first of all the best in our own people. One can still see and admire this in some of the peasant populations of Europe, and in the new spiritual awakening of Germany. But bad feeding makes unhealthy, restless, internally quarrelsome people, always ready to be swayed without fixed purpose. If one quotes the vigour, health and beauty of certain European mountaineers and peasants, or if one quotes the magnificent example of the Hunza hillmen in India or even the Chinese and Japanese peasantry, one is continually faced with the petulant answer: " Oh, they are nearer the animals and we are civilized, so there must be a difference." [1]

The inference can only be that with all the wisdom and loftiness of progress and civilization

[1] Merry England was no romantic conception of the Golden Age. Unbiased foreign observers in the sixteenth century were continually remarking on the beauty and contentment of our people as being outstanding in Europe. But in the nineteenth century Heine asks, on seeing the Londoner, what our rulers have been doing to make such an ugly race.

we take ill health, restlessness and discontent as our proud burden, and not as our shame. There is undoubtedly undernourishment of too large a portion of our people. But even when there is no work it is far greater than it should be. We have probably spent £2,000,000,000 since 1900 on compulsory education and yet the result is that the standard of housekeeping in general has gone from bad to miserable. What a record of false standards goes with this boasted education! Among eleven million who signed the peace ballot perhaps one hundred thousand know how to produce internal peace for their own bodies. In the face of almost overwhelming complacency we must try to recover with intellectual effort now what is the immemorial experience of the happy peoples. It is worth while and it is the only road to lasting salvation, for the root of health lies in the soil.

Writing in this connection Sir Robert McCarrison says: "It may therefore be accepted as an axiom that the greatest single factor in the production of good health is the right kind of food, and the greatest single factor in the production of ill health is the wrong kind of food."

If we eat a balanced meal that comes from healthy soil we will have all the food values and the vitamins known and unknown which our bodies need. But it will not avail us if the soil be impoverished or the system of agriculture faulty, just as all the capsuled vitamins on the market can only palliate our ills if we do not eat wisely. The

healthiest peoples are those which take most care
for their agriculture, which return to the land its
own waste products, and which look upon land not
as a means of exploitation, but as the centre of
their own life. The food we eat to-day has no
such guarantee. This aspect of health will be
examined in another chapter, but it is one which
makes the regeneration of our own lands a prime
concern. The stock of this island has gone out
to the perimeters of the world. It has been human
stock, cattle and seed; wherever it has gone and
been wisely chosen, it has improved the standard
of products on the lands to which it went. This
proves the fundamental healthy fertility of these
islands.

Again and again those who have bought our
agricultural stock have to come back to us to re-
new it, since on foreign soil the blood deteriorates.
Professor Stapledon is to-day showing the vast
superiority of our indigenous grasses to imported
grass seeds in the plant world. From Agincourt to
the nineteenth century, our men abroad were the
terror of their enemies, and the leaders of those
who were their friends. If our stock improves the
stock of other lands, but deteriorates in a few
generations abroad, and if these islands have in the
past sent leaders to the outer world to an extent
undreamed of since Roman days, is it too much to
suppose that the land of England had something to
do with this? If to-day we rely—and have for nearly
three generations relied—on the foreign lands for

86

the bulk of the people's food, is it far-fetched to wonder if this has not played its part in our national deterioration? It is true that a decline in the reproduction of our best human stocks, and an increase in the reproduction of our poorest has played an even greater part in our deterioration, but we have not had the advantage of our own soil even to mitigate the effects. The war seems almost to have been a dying flash. For magnificently as people responded to the country's need, and endured till the war's end, we suffered less and had to show no more stamina than others. Since then we have watched an Empire crumble, and our utmost consolation in leadership has been to see Mr. Eden and his predecessors flitter from capital to capital as Genevan *Madones des Sleepings*.

CHAPTER VI

WASTE LANDS AND NEW SAHARAS

P ART ONE outlined the dangers into which
modern machinery and modern methods of
warfare, and modern transport have led us. They
are all dangers which are temporary and which can
be rectified to some extent by emergency measures
such as armaments, fuel reserves, and food reserves.
But there is another danger that will demand the
utmost patience and foresight to overcome, and
which makes an expanding home agriculture a
necessity. This is world erosion, which is contracting world food supplies. In other days, when
transport worked by sail and pack animal, it was
very difficult to exploit one part of the world for
the sake of other parts, and so deserts were
localized. But even so, when nations crumbled
it was the land that wasted with them. The great
prehistoric migrations that peopled the West and
India with Aryan stock left behind the vast wastes
of Gobi; Mesopotamia is deemed to have been
the parent of the Mediterranean civilization. But
to-day upon the banks of crumbled canals archaeo-
logists dig through layer on layer of lost cities
buried in the sands, and agriculture forms only

narrow strips along the great rivers. The lost and desert cities of India and Arabia excite our wonder and people our imagination. But that is all. Nearer to our own time we know that the Northern Sahara was once the granary of Rome. Mussolini's colonization there is the effort to wrest inch by inch from desert the lost territory of the sown. Hundreds of years ago Doge Dandolo impounded a crusading army for the sack of Constantinople, but to do so he had to build a fleet to carry Christendom's array. So to build ships he cut the forests along the Dalmatian coasts. From that day until this it has been desert for all to see.

These examples show two reasons for desert. The first is insecurity which makes for bad farming and the disrepair of canals and irrigation works. The borders of desert and sown are always infested by Nomad bands which mean looting and cattle-lifting. Without defence there are few cattle, and the blistered crops edge backwards as the desert advances. The humus goes from the land and dust storms blow it hither and yon. Whatever rain may fall succeeds in eroding the fertility that remains. To-day the Canary Islands are being continually enriched by Sahara dust. The other reason for the desert is the failure to appreciate that not only are trees and green fodder crops continuous makers of moisture, but they prevent erosion by their roots and they enrich the earth crust with minerals in organic form which they have drawn from below. This is how deserts were made in the past and how

89

they are growing now. They are the fruits of
man's greatest sin against himself and all living
things; they embalm the mummies of past glory,
and will in turn close over the entire world if we
do not act before it is too late.

Transport to-day is making more deserts than
ever Nomad raiders or ambitious Doges of the
past could do. Modern mass production has increased the population of Europe and Asia.
Cheaper labour of every race and colour is needed,
and cheap labour needs cheaper food. So the railways and ships of the world ply to and fro with
the products of exploited labour in exchange for
the products of exploited land. Sand comes to
African grass lands so that niggers can buy
bicycles. The Gulf of Mexico is turbid with the
rich soil of Indiana and Ohio so that the steel
works of Pittsburg and cotton gins of Lancashire
may flourish. The forests of Siberia are felled so
that Russia may pay interest. These generaliza-
tions are essentially true.

America and Canada are the two countries in
which the process of exploiting virgin land has
gone furthest. This process is more the direct outcome of the industrial revolution than anything
else. Now the excuse for the immediate repeal of
the Corn Laws was the Irish famine. Yet while
Ireland was starving, in the ports of Ireland grain
ships were being loaded for export; the potato crop
had failed after harvest, and the peasants could not
buy the products of Irish land. There was no

acute general grain shortage, but at the time industry was paying for corn at just prices (prices which would have been even more just had the farm labourer been paid a decent wage). The one thing that mattered to the industrialist and indeed to the spirit of the time, was cheap labour. The great God-intimate Manchester school made much of cheap breakfast tables, but protested bitterly that coal-mining and industry would be ruined if child labour were not available at ten hours a day above and below ground. All the old hypocrites really wanted was cheap labour to find easy markets for their produce. The Napoleonic wars had put money into their hands, and so they won. Instead of adjusting wages and prices to decent levels for everyone, they upset the balance between land and industry. This upsetting of the balance went further, for by ruining the landlord, squire and yeoman, it deprived the people of potential champions and leaders. The industrial snowball of debt, misery and exploitation began; if it was to continue cheap food was essential. In those days English labour, though worse treated than now, had not been infected with the slave virus which another three generations of cheap labour was to engender. There was a limit beyond which men would not submit. Social legislations to dope men against fundamental political ills was to come later. Revolution in the latter part of the nineteenth century was staved off by the cheap wheat of the new world.

Whatever the rugged virtues of the pioneer he was no respecter of the soil. No followers of Jenghiz Khan raped the virgins of Samarkand as thoroughly as the pioneer raped the virgin soil. Having exhausted one spot he moved west to rape again. For thousands of years the Mississippi Valley had been peopled only by wandering Nomads, buffaloes, grass, and the presence of God. In that time nature had stored a gold-mine of fertility in the prairies, partly by erosion deposited in the valley from the forest-clad ranges, and partly by grass year after year returning its organic humus to the soil. When the plough was put into this land, for almost nothing it yielded heavy crops. Cotton and maize in the South; wheat, maize and barley in the North. But in a land of fierce extremes of heat and cold, when the surface of the soil was worked loose and thin, it could not withstand the action of wind and rain. Heavy rains carried the humus—which is the lightest part of the soil—down to the sea, and wind blew it upwards. There was no grass and covering of roots to hold it. In some places—especially in the North—trees were cut to clear the land for the plough; in others, near the mountains, whole forests were laid low to sell as timber, while man's carelessness burnt grass and forest which were as yet untouched. It is said to take 400 years for Nature to make an inch of topsoil, but man can waste it in two decades. In a world so wide land seemed limitless, waste and carelessness excusable. Voices were raised against the unregulated felling of timber which was not replanted, but this was for fear of a future shortage of timber, not for its effect on the land.

There was always a new horizon to seek when land had been exhausted. The virgin lands were rarely home, for all the home-town boosting. They were the means of making a fortune, not of creating a homestead. Wheat would sell, so wheat was grown and the straw burnt, while livestock and green fodder crops were not an integral part of the balanced farm economy. Napoleon's soldiers had a marshal's baton in their knapsack; the covered wagons held a million dollars, or a nomad's urge.

California for a generation has been the happy hunting-ground of retired farmers and 'cow punchers' pitching horseshoes in the sun. But to-day there is a new class seeking asylum. *The Times* New York correspondent in the issue of July 19th, 1937, under the heading " Middle West 'Dust Bowl' Refugees ", says:

70,000 IN CALIFORNIAN " SHANTY TOWNS "

A conference presided over by the Governor of California will be held next Tuesday at Bakersfield, California, to consider problems presented by the settlement in the great fruit-growing areas, the San Joaquin Valley, of 70,000 refugees from the Middle West's " dust bowl ".

These refugees, without means to construct proper

houses, are living in " shanty towns ", in huts made of anything that will help to shelter them, from pieces of wooden packing-cases and odd bits of galvanized iron to corrugated cardboard. Sanitary conditions are so bad that there have been three outbreaks of typhoid fever in these " shanty towns ". Moreover, many of the refugees are close to starvation, local relief agencies having exhausted their means of taking care of them.

This ' dust bowl ' is no accident of nature, no seismic cataclysm such as engulfed Atlantis. It is man's handiwork. After the pioneers passed the land was filled. But the spirit remained the same— it was the spirit of exploitation and with it was still a general ignorance of good husbandry. The disproportion of the awards between industry and agriculture emphasized the bad farming. The Middle West became the interest slaves of the financial East, especially after the federal reserve system of banking came in. The wider banking risks are spread the less the banker cares for local interests. There is no democracy, but only three main classes in the western world to-day : the wage slave, the interest slave, and the plutocrat.

Thus the Middle Western farmer has ceased to exploit land for himself, he has had to exploit it to pay interest. Often the farmer, having exhausted his soil, has tried to repair the loss, not by the relatively costly business of good mixed farming, but by artificial manures. Appropriately enough, the artificial manure-maker is the manufacturer of

94

high explosives, so what he gains on the swings of war he can keep on the roundabouts of peace. The reckless use of artificial manure is as destructive as the careless handling of explosives. In the spirit of the profit age nearly all agricultural research has been towards bigger and better exploitation of the land rather than saner and sounder farming. The key-note has been to make the land give more and take less. This was accelerated by the famine prices of foodstuff in the war and just afterwards. And when the slump came it was more necessary than ever for farmers to survive.

Artificial manures may be useful in exceptional cases to stimulate production, or as with basic slag to help derelict grass land, but unless they are used in conjunction with good farming they are highly dangerous. The processes of life depend as much on decay as on growth. Healthy growth can only take place when there has been proper decay of organic matter which becomes humus. This can only be brought about by the working of soil bacteria. Reckless use of sulphate of ammonia, nitro chalk, potash and other salts kill these bacteria, and so the plant cannot remain healthy when there is no humus in the soil. Thus the overdosing of badly farmed soil with artificial manure can complete the ruin which the endless cereal crops and cutting of forests has started.

When there are no trees and not enough grass, lucerne or clover on the land, there is not enough moisture in the air for rain to fall in the hot summer season. Moreover, when the land has been continuously ploughed under these conditions, it is in very fine particles, the lightest of which is the humus on the surface. The first high wind creates a dust storm which removes the particles of essential humus from the land, bares the roots of the growing crop, and covers the leaves with dust, which makes it impossible for the leaves to breathe properly. Thus added to drought one gets undernourished crops growing in the worst conditions. Crops in such conditions get disease like human beings. We read that the relatively promising wheat crop of 1937 in U.S.A. and Canada suffered from the black rust, the spores of which blew so that hitherto unaffected areas were diseased. If the crops were really healthy the rust would not seriously damage them, since the spores from unhealthy crops have always blown. Disease fastens on unhealthy growth. So even in a favourable year bad land will not generally yield a good harvest.

That is one side of the gold medal for prize folly. The other comes in early spring. Floods in the Mississippi basin have become a commonplace. The illustrated papers and the Gaumont Graphic show us houses in Louisville with people rescued by boat from upper windows, and America rings with appeals for flood victims. These are again not an act of God, but of man's hand. Soil which has no humus and no trees ceases to be porous. One can walk over it with eyes shut and feel one is on concrete. Water no longer penetrates into the subsoil to become a reservoir against drought in the summer. It runs off the surface, carrying with it the top soil and the humus on the land into the ocean where it is lost for ever. So the process of desert-making goes on in winter and summer as well. In winter it drowns, while in summer it starves.

Although there is a growing consciousness of something wrong, the right treatment has not yet started. A forest belt many miles wide for hundreds of miles has been attempted through the heart of the dust bowl, but it has failed because, when a Sahara has been made, you cannot reclaim it from the centre but only from the edge, or by pushing outwards from oases. In the meantime, the edge of the dust bowl is advancing outwards by forty miles a year in places, and about 2000 farms are being lost annually. Hence the above paragraph from *The Times* is all part of the tale. There is no doubt that the larger the area becomes the more formidable are its effects on the cultivatable edges. Canada is suffering not only from bad husbandry, but from bad neighbourhood. For the first time in a generation the 1937 wheat harvest was estimated to be so bad that she would not have enough wheat to feed Great Britain and herself. As in the U.S.A. so in Canada will good years produce more than to-day, in spite of the dust bowl and bad farming, but no amount of

G 97

'sophistication'[1] of news will serve to hide the
fact that the years of bad crop production in summer and floods in winter are due to bad farming,
and the consequent increase of desert land.

The Americans can no longer produce vast surplus stores of wheat and other cereals. In general,
the only traditionally well-farmed land in temperate North America is the land farmed by the
French-Canadian peasants of Canada, where a
peasant population and wise mixed farming has
for two hundred years kept the land in sound
heart, which in itself should be sufficient lesson.
Thus the first fruits of easy profits and exploitation are writ large across a new continent. If the
old world had not needed cheap food for the industrial revolution a very different story in English
history might have been written, but cheap transport and cheap industrial labour have gone hand
in hand. From 1800 to 1913 world trade increased
twenty times in value.

The evil effect has not rested there. In the
U.S.A., as in Canada, there has been a large movement from country to towns. The rewards of industry have been greater than the rewards of
husbandry, so the balance has been upset in the
urban favour. The U.S.A. is now an importer of
foodstuffs,[2] and we have the fantastic picture of an

[1] See recent articles in *The Times* to prove all is best in the
best of all possible western worlds.

[2] See W. S. Haldane's letter to *The Times* on December
22nd, 1937.

underpopulated country, originally having immense possibilities, unable for the moment to feed itself.

But if this were the whole story we need not fear overmuch. The overpopulated old world shows the same symptoms exaggerated a hundred-fold. West of Russia the population of Europe has grown so rapidly in urban conditions that there is not enough land to feed the people by western methods of agriculture.

South American agriculture has so far escaped most, but not all of the devastating results of bad farming in North America. But we must remember that she is now producing not only meat herself, but large quantities of food which is being processed into animal products in Europe. The shortage ultimately will be in animals as well.

New Zealand is a great reservoir for animal foodstuffs. As islands, her rainfall is less affected by de-afforestation than if she were a continent. Yet even in New Zealand there are signs of serious erosion through grazing on steep slopes and too much interference with the natural vegetation. But reports from New Zealand show consciousness of the trouble and determination to deal with it. All the same, it is unlikely that New Zealand will be an increasing source of food unless the country is farmed much more on far eastern methods than on lines of western exploitation.

Australia, a sub-continent the size of the U.S.A., has little over 5,000,000 inhabitants. But it is comparable to the Sahara surrounded by its fringes of cultivation plus the Nile Valley. When we remember that a common method of obtaining farm land there has been to ring the trees so that these died and clearings could be made for the plough, there is little hope of increasing agricultural production there, rather it is the reverse. Unless Australia is rapidly turned into a peasant country ruin of the soil is inevitable. At present well over half the meagre population is in the towns. The reported problems from Australia show a really desperate position. In many cases the rainfall and the conditions obtaining one hundred years ago made the greatest care necessary. The plough and the grazing have each unconsciously intensified the desert. Taking an objective view, it is hard to feel anything but pessimism for the general future of Australian soil. Funds for reclamation of man-made desert are small, and Australia is already much over-urbanized. Even for a European country her percentage of rural population would be dangerously low. The only hope for such lands would be fixed peasant types of cultivation and grazing.

It is first and foremost man's labour and not his use of machinery that eats into the desert, nowhere so much as on the land has machinery without control made itself the master of man. So far machinery has been designed to exploit rather than to help the land. If hand-reaping and horse-ploughing had prevailed there would have been

·very little dust bowl in America, as mixed farming would have been necessary.

In the southern hemisphere only Africa south of the equator remains. Here again ' progress ' has ·upset the balance of labour. Two things have happened; the ' pacification ' of the native and the encouragement to export so that the nigger can buy bicycles or wireless or clothes, and so help European industry. When missionaries, for instance, come to darkest Africa they have been horrified, as in the South Sea Islands, by the natives' ' godless ' but healthy custom of wearing no clothes. It is doubtful if this puritanism could have so much effect were it not that trade follows the trouser. Men unused to trousers and women to Mother Hubbards do not weave them from their own soil products, they buy them from the factory. At one stroke they acquire ' godliness '. and an appetite for industrial products. Virtue then becomes not its own reward, but the results of field labour. So the plough is introduced on the hill slopes and monoculture of. crops takes place. What follows is sheet erosion—the quickest and worst form of erosion. This form of erosion is taking place on sloping land the world over, unless that land is terraced. The early British terraces of our forefathers show that they were wiser farmers than ourselves. The old African native method of farming is mixed crop culture, which in England is called dredge corn. This native method covers the ground with a variety of crops which intermingles roots and cereals. Not only does this make the growth of crops complementary, but by root and leaf covering of the earth makes erosion by wind and rain less possible. For economic reasons we have introduced monoculture, where each plant competes with its neighbour and so exhausts the soil more in particular constituents. By the use of plough instead of mattock, and drill instead of broadcasting, we have let in the action of wind and rain. The economic returns from cotton have in many parts of Africa produced the worst type of monoculture in time as well as space. That is, the same crop is grown year after year on the same ground. Monoculture is as bad for the land in orchard-growing as it is in field agriculture. This is taking place not only in South Africa, but in all the fruit-growing areas of the world from Palestine to Oregon.

In general and under present conditions where the plough is drawn in Africa the shadow of the desert runs before it. This is not all. Miss Huxley's article in *The Times* of June 11th, 1937, shows how the grazing land is losing heart. Here again we have upset the balance of nature. Where there is cotton, for instance, there is not enough dung and alternation of fodder crops; where there is grazing there are too many animals. The goat which has been banished by a careful Mussolini from Italy is increasing by leaps and bounds in Africa. The missionary has denounced the sacrifice of goats as unchristian, he forgets that the scapegoat is a household world of Bible origin. So the goat increases unchecked by ritual and with the locust eats every living piece of green. Cattle which tribal raids, warfare, and nomad habits once kept in check are too thick on the grazing lands, now tribes are settled and unable to enjoy a foray. Moreover, we have checked cattle diseases and tsetse-fly, and so land on which grass is eaten out becomes like the ploughed field—a prey to wind and rain.

Even with the most energetic action, which must be both wise and far-seeing, there is little hope in Africa to increase food supplies for a generation. What is far more likely is that the desert will grow apace for a generation before a desperate and sadder but wiser world takes it in hand. Countries and even continents, just as much as individual farmers, must be balanced between forest and farm, grass and plough. When a continent becomes unbalanced by a shortage of forest, whole countries become desert as the water table and river flow change.

Only Asia remains wherein to find comfort. There things are not only difficult, but immediately dangerous. Over half the world's population is in Asia living on the very edge of subsistence for the most part, and casting hungry eyes across the oceans.

Japan is now industrialized and needs even for her people more food than she can grow, amazing as her thrifty cultivation is. China and Korea and parts of Mongolia are likewise cultivating each inch of soil and saving each particle of waste. Agriculture there has reached an intensive pitch unknown in Europe. The Far East has for thousands of years been in this state.[1] Here again, modern industry is breeding new populations from her swarming millions that will need the food of more lands to feed them. The west has not only brought industry but civil war as well, by which the land together with the peasants have suffered. To civil war invasion has now been added and the overflow of population in years to come will be greater than ever.

In India we have increased the population by more millions than the years gone by since the battle of Plassey. We have put millions of acres under cultivation by irrigation, but we have checked pestilence and stopped famine. The population has no natural limitations. Moreover, irrigation, unless well understood and wisely used, breeds famine in the end. When irrigated land gets waterlogged or eroded, the last state of the land is worse than the first. The use of water has already been reckless and crops have far too often been used for sale of the land and not for subsistence. Fuel shortage has turned dung into the hearth fire and not the compost heap. Now that the administration is deteriorating under so-called self-government, irrigation will become more and more dangerous. Modern India has all the seeds of the

[1] See *Farmers of Forty Centuries*, by F. H. King.

world's greatest famine latent in the soil, although she still has seeds of plenty if these could be cultivated. Modern implements, westernized large-scale husbandry, artificial manures on the plantation system will almost certainly cultivate the seeds of famine as they have elsewhere the world over.

Persia, Afghanistan and Asia Minor offer no immediate hope to feed the outside world, not even from the citrus groves of Palestine.

There remains only the U.S.S.R. The possibilities of agricultural development are enormous, but the potentialities of famine are greater. A vast land area is always drier than a sea-bordered land. Therefore the greatest care in forest conservation is required to keep the balance of moisture. Africa, for instance, has 10 instead of 30 per cent. for its area in forest, and so the Sahara grows. Russia and Siberia are no exceptions to this rule. " The hushed Khorasmian waste " was once fertile land and the Aral and the Caspian were once far vaster seas. Since the war Russia has been exploiting timber to pay debt interest. Her timber reserves, from the supply point of view, may be nearly limitless, but as timber is a conserver of moisture, she needs each stick, including replacements of the felled trees and increase elsewhere. Moreover, she has had to exploit agricultural land to dump wheat on the world. It has not only paid for debts, it has been the cause of a depressed and overloaded world market. In order to carry on this policy,

ten years ago most of her livestock was killed off
or starved as insufficient fodder was left. At the
same time the Kulaks, her best farmers and
soundest peasant stock, were killed or exiled to the
timber camps.

The Big Idea, the apogee of Americanism, has
become God to the Russian. Not only does he
have the world's largest power-station, but he
must have the world's largest farms and fields.
Collectivized farming is the order of the day. But
collectivized farming in the Russian sense is almost
certain to mean bad husbandry. Wheat fields of
hundreds or thousands of acres in the end mean
a new dust bowl. At present the United States
has the world's largest failure in farming, but
Russia, in this also, will ultimately have the record.
Already experts in Russia are busy discussing
sheet erosion which has been found to occur on
slopes with a fall as small as one in thirty-three.
With the use of huge monoculture crop areas,
drills and big machinery, this is bound to get worse
and worse. Only a balanced peasant cultivation
and afforestation can prevent it. Meanwhile, the
population of Russia grows while her lands de-
teriorate.

Europe already cannot supply her own needs,
and the world, which a decade ago seemed limitless, is contracting like a sucked orange before our
eyes. Europe, too, has suffered from exploitation
of the land. Everywhere the big machine is coming
in and the large field is taking the place of the

peasant holding. Nowhere in the world has the use of artificial manure been so general for so long a time, and yet the crop production of Europe has been contracting little by little after the first initial rise thirty years ago.

The peasant has been forced to pay more taxes and to sell off more from the land, while for the same reason the great estates have been mechanized. The destruction of forest caused by the war has not yet been made good. Germany, the greatest user of artificial manures, is suffering now from a series of bad harvests. Plants and animals are preys to increasingly severe attacks of endemic disease and pests.

THE POSITION IN OUR OWN ISLAND

But there is one form of waste that is at present largely confined to the Occident, which is very serious in a crowded world. It might be described as the " Urban Progress " Desert. In England we have been particularly reckless in increasing it. Professor Stapledon mentions it in his book, *The Land*, since when it has been growing by leaps and bounds. The geology of the urban desert has infinite variations; sometimes it is tarmac, sometimes housing schemes in half-timber, public buildings in brick and stone, sometimes human bones, sometimes water reservoirs, and sometimes the steel, concrete and glass of factories, sometimes refuse dumps and sewage farms. Sometimes it is merely effluent from factories which poison fish, but in nearly every case it is a permanent loss to agriculture and food production. Now some of this 'progress' may be necessary and even healthy, but in other cases it is unnecessary and wasteful. But it has this common denominator, that in every case it is done without the slightest regard for our scanty agricultural land reserves in this country. Not only does it amount in the aggregate to hundreds of thousands of acres, but it is inclined to take the best land and not the worst land.

There is also a second source of loss from 'progress' which, if not permanent, is none the less serious. That is the loss of agricultural land to aerodromes, playing-fields, and golf-courses. Such things as hard tennis courts and car parks are permanent losses, slight in themselves, but all mounting up to swell the total devoted to tarmac and graveyards. A majority of the great urban centres are on flat river lands which are the most valuable for agricultural purposes. From Battersea to Esher there runs a strip of alluvial market-garden land as valuable as any garden land in the world. Four intensive crops a year can be taken from it, if properly farmed, without hurting the soil. If Mussolini guts an Alp for the rebuilding of Milan, it is small loss either to mountain, agriculture, or Milanese plain. But if we dig gravel by the Great West Road and disembowel bricks from the soil near Peterborough, we not only

destroy so much land in the process, but we then
proceed to smear tawdry bricks and concrete like
rancid margarine on the best land of Britain. The
destruction of market-garden land along the Great
West Road for factories and housing schemes is
criminal waste, wherein the only result is to create
new slums, new traffic problems, and greater loss
of nervous energy among those who have to travel
to and fro from work. We have not conserved
or built upwards, we have only sprawled outwards
till the home counties are one vast suburb. There
would have been some excuse if we had taken the
waste heaths adjacent instead of the best land, or
the heavy clay hills of Hertfordshire and chalk
uplands, all of which would have been healthier
for the people involved than the low-lying river
lands.

In England the most criminal disregard of
agriculture in a single example is the compulsory
purchase by the Metropolitan Water Board of Mr.
Secrett's land at Walton-on-Thames. Here were
200 acres under heavy and continuous crops
of first-class vegetables, with a correspond-
ing quantity of direct and indirect labour at
good pay upon it. It was land not only in the
highest state of healthy fertility with irrigation
plants and packing houses, but it possessed the
most valuable private horticultural experimental
station in England; and one station of this sort is
worth a dozen Government stations. All this is
being ruined to provide a water reservoir so

people can bathe and wash cars in time of drought. It was not only waste of land but a waste of experience and constructive work. One can begin again but only from agricultural zero, no matter what the compensation may be. Mr. Secrett's case is just a glaring example. The waste and purchase, compulsory and otherwise, of land from Battersea to Esher has deprived London of one of its nearest and healthiest sources of fresh vegetables, and it has deprived England of the skill of thousands of hereditary market gardeners, greenfingered craftsmen, by a combination of blind shortsightedness, cupidity, and stupidity.

Although it is impossible to estimate accurately, we have probably lost nearly a million acres of potentially good food-growing land in this and other ways since the war. The road policy has likewise been one of incredible waste. Wherever new arterial roads have been built or widened, the fence land has been set back many yards on each side, which has meant in the aggregate an enormous waste of ground, nearly all of which is good pasture and arable, for the most part in valley land. Not only have we preferred oil to coal to encourage heavy and light motor transport, but we have accentuated the waste in duplication of existing transport schemes by wasting land. A building line along the roads is a wise precaution, but a new wide fence-line, until such becomes necessary, is sheer folly, and involves the spread of weeds and unproductive labour to keep weeds down. The policy of building service roads parallel to the public road in all housing development in the country is another unwarrantable waste of land when coupled with set-back road boundaries.

It is more than doubtful if western water sanitation is the wisest form for urban health. But this involves a destruction of good land in sewage farms. When we consider the enormous quantities of food consumed in Britain we should by its manurial value alone be the most fertile country in the world. Instead of which it and most of our home-grown food waste are either dumped into the sea or used to destroy land with sewage farms rather than to fertilize it. If such a thing happened in the healthy populations of China or Japan they would starve. Once when there was a large horse population in our cities the manure this made did return to the soil, but now that industry has 'progressed' the horse cannot keep pace. Therein also the land is robbed and the nation's economy becomes more and more unbalanced.

Perhaps the most serious, because the most incalculable form of land robbery that has gone on, comes from the system of water supply. Most of England's seaside is a town. In and about London alone over a quarter of our population is centred. Modern sanitation requires hitherto inconceivable quantities of water for bath, basin and lavatory alone. Every night London streets are hosed

down, every day half a million cars and lorries are
washed with a probable average of well over 100
gallons of water per vehicle. The majority of
these vehicles are washed near the sea.

Hundreds of new factories around London and
the South Coast have their own deep well bore-
holes, using millions of gallons daily in addition
to the public water supplies. Thus by far the
greatest quantity of water which is drawn from
the land for town and industry is poured straight
into the sea. The increase of intensive cultivation,
which is possible, is limited by the water table of
the land. Such a reckless use of fresh water is just
as dangerous as cutting down a nation's forests.
This use of water shows no signs of abating, but
rather it appears steadily to increase. Every year,
when there is a drought, earnest and well-meaning
addle-brains shout that 'progress' demands that
we have a national water grid. Nothing could be
more dangerous for the future. It is bad enough
already when we have City Water Boards seeking
new supplies outside their own catchment areas. It
is one thing to sink bore-holes for use in the
countryside where the waste runs back into the soil
and does good; it is quite another to draw off
water from one area to another where it is not
even returned to the soil but poured directly into
the sea, or indirectly by river into the sea. The
bore-holes, for instance, which water Southampton
are probably robbing the underground rivers many
miles inland. As each year goes by the springs re-

treat from the old head-waters, and even the old winterbournes cease to run in winter. On the reverse side also, all areas impermeable to rain cause waste in conservation and flood in storm periods. Little of the rain which falls on London gets into the soil, and the same applies to road surfaces in these islands which accentuates the problem both of flood and water conservation.

Perhaps England has the most glaring cases of waste of land of one sort and another. But this form of waste is going on all over Europe. In Germany, in spite of hundreds of thousands of hectares having been reclaimed, probably double this area has been taken up for roads and aerodromes and building schemes. But in every country where industry has developed and urban populations have heavily overbalanced rural population, the water utilization is bound to become more and more serious from the agricultural point of view. This reckless use of water will have a cumulative effect on limiting potential agricultural production. Thus greater New York alone requires the rain capture from watersheds covering 900 square miles, or a depth of six feet of water in 200 square miles.[1] What this means in loss to soil is almost incalculable.

This chapter indicates that without a radical change in agricultural practice and concerted world attempts to halt erosion and to regenerate deserts, the spectre of famine will materialize into a reality

[1] See *Nations Can Live at Home*, by O. W. Wilcox, p. 152.

without the aid of war. This alone constitutes an urgent and imperative reason for storing reserves of food in any form that animals and human beings alike consume. Such a reserve will not only be of the utmost value in war, but as food supplies shorten in peace time it will enable us to have some breathing space in which to re-organize our own agricultural production and restore fertility to our fields until we reach a point where by careful rationing we could be self-supporting.

But even so we will, in common with all Occidental nations, require to guard our remaining soil from the reckless intrusion of urban methods in building, road-making, and water usage. If ever there was a time for thinking agronomically it is the present.

PART IV
Regeneration

They shall return as Strangers
They shall remain as Sons.

RUDYARD KIPLING

INTRODUCTION

MEN desire to cheat death; it is the very instinct that makes for the survival of our species. In our own bodies we cannot do so. But if we can leave a sounder stock of children to follow us with hope that they will survive and flourish, we will have cheated death. This small flame of instinct has burnt low and the sound stocks are perishing. Not even safety in war will save us unless we serve the soil from which we are fashioned. Indeed it were better for cataclysm quickly to overtake us rather than to die by inches.

So with credits in the city, with the necessary material of battle by air and land and water, and even with rations of food stores against emergency, we can only put off for a decade or a generation the fate which comes to all nations which are too soft and which protect the evil and the unsound in their midst at the expense of the best. Yet there is sound stock left. If the majority of our aristocracy has sold its birthright for photography without dignity, comfort without responsibility, and meals without payment; if our squires have been wiped out, and if the middle classes have rallied to a money standard, there is among artisans and working men of England the good stock left that makes England the pivot of western civilization. If we dissolve this stock the regenerate nations cannot save Europe. If we regenerate the land we can give hope to the sound stocks and increase the health of all. It is the sound who will return to the soil, not the weakling or the parasite. Men will desire to defend their inheritance of flourishing homesteads, where they would be indifferent to the fate of a conveyor belt and the shining new concrete rabbit warrens of flats where they now lodge.

In loving service to the soil men see each season how death may be cheated and learn how they must always protect the sound seed from the weeds, and how close breeding makes fine types of stock. In towns they learn always how the sound stock must tend the weeds, how the cross breeds multiply and batten on the breeds of English culture. In towns they learn how cunning and slickness are qualities to make for fitness to survive; they do not learn that if the best are to survive it must be by careful tending and protection from weeds and parasites. If only to relearn this ancient lesson, regeneration of the soil must come before national revival. Love for the living and the unborn generations of the sound must come before pity for the misfits and the botched, and replace admiration for the nimble-witted parasite with well-lined pockets and no care for the future.

118

REGENERATION

A nation will only survive with a purpose which is to cheat death by building for the future and working in the present for those policies which ensure health, independence, and the culture of sound breeds.

So while armaments and food reserves may be necessary as insurance policies against immediate disaster, a regeneration of agriculture is the first policy which we must contemplate for such insurance to have meaning.

CHAPTER VII

SKELETON OF THE HOMELAND

BEFORE we can proceed to show that the land may be our salvation, it is necessary to analyse the causes of the decline of home agriculture and to examine its present status. The land is in a bad state for two reasons: the lets and hindrances of the State socialism we now enjoy, and the need to exploit land the world over in order to exploit cheaply fed labour at the cheapest wage. The State socialism is the direct outcome of the exploitation of labour, that is, of giving men a contract to live by being exploited and not a status in life. Palliatives can ease the conscience of the exploiter as well as hide the truth from the exploited.

We have seen how up till 1914 there was a very real residue of fertility in the soil. In general, the standard of farming was good for the land, even if it was not up to 'economic standards'.

It was, in fact, based on reality and not the financiers' conception of economics, which is to treat all men and all live things (including the earth itself) as inanimate chattels. Moreover, the landlord for a few years after Mr. Lloyd George's famous budget had not been taxed quite beyond the point of maintenance. Low rents in the great arable districts had not entirely driven the squire, who depended on land, out of existence; and while men had money invested elsewhere they could still preserve land as an amenity which, if it did not pay, at any rate did not represent a serious loss. It was a pernicious system, since it drove the land-owner to business instead of caring personally for his land, and so deprived the country of independent leadership.

The war came. It meant that land had to be exploited sometimes under the direction of ignorant shirkers in Whitehall to feed the people. In many instances those who owned land were killed. Their heirs paid death duties and thus helped on the ruin of the countryside for which they had fought. It meant also that all repairs to cottages, buildings, drains, and fences fell into arrears. Partly to pay death duties one-third of the land changed hands after the war, mostly to tenants who had a new and inflexible landlord in the bank. Hence, old landlords and new owner-occupiers were too impoverished to set about the repairs necessary after the deflation set in. Even semi-fixed charges like tithe and land tax became an intolerable incubus instead of a barely tolerable burden in the arable districts. Labour costs grew out of all proportion to returns, low as agricultural wages seemed compared to industrial wages. So for tenant and owner alike, dispensing with labour was the only alternative to bankruptcy. Land is not like a conveyor belt, and the best fertilizer is human sweat.

Since 1925 this position has never seriously altered. Retail prices for foodstuffs stood by 1935 at one-third above those of 1914, while retail prices for other essential commodities had risen by nearly three-quarters of their 1914 value[1]. Of all trades in the world since the war the retail trade has consistently flourished and expanded. The share prices of the United Dairies, and the great chain stores, many of which have grown out of one small shop in the last twenty years, all reflect the abundant prosperity of the middleman in a time of dearth for producers. Thus it is certain that the land has suffered out of all proportion even in comparison with the figures shown for retail prices.

The improvement in rural wages and housing conditions was long overdue and is welcome just as good airy cowsheds are an integral part of clean milk production, but neither have been related to the national balance of life. The result has been that a quarter of a million workers have been driven from the land since 1921. This does not include the numbers lost by a reduction in estate staff which is all part of employment on the land. Thus in a period when a large increase of labour to make good the repairs to fertility and neglected buildings caused by the war was required, the

[1] See N.F.U. Information Service, April 1937, *Why Always Food?*

land has suffered by losing some 30 per cent. of its servants.

The exploitation of land in Great Britain and the completely free ingress of foreign food is only to be expected from Britain's financial record. Great Britain, as the world's foremost moneylender, has strained every nerve to keep London as the world's financial centre. The return to the gold standard cost the producers of this country £2,000,000,000 in dead weight of debt at one stroke of the pen, but it made the world safe for banking—for the time being. Thus in order to make sure that our foreign investments are safe, we have kept the world's market open for food in Great Britain. Other countries not so industrialized have taken measures to preserve their agriculture. The result has been that we take in such things as beef and butter the vast majority of the world's exports. When there is such a relatively limited market as Great Britain only open to the world, the extra surplus of one commodity in one country brings down the general world price for this commodity at once. This in turn depresses the price of other staple foods. As there is hardly ever any country that has not got a temporary glut of some food commodity, the price is permanently depressed to a point below the costs of production. Thus apart from foreign subsidies and in many cases cheaper foreign labour, and apart from the capital realization in the fertility of virgin lands, since transport and refrigeration have developed, the free market in

123

Great Britain has almost always meant that our own farmers have had to sell under, or at the world cost of production; for it is quite clear that none of this loss has been borne by the distributor. In fact, the distributor has generally kept retail prices fairly steady, while he bargained down the producer on the strength of surplus imports. It is not only the profit of the distributor that is reflected in this ability to create prosperity out of the adversity of others, it is also his improvements in capital out of income, namely the buying up of the small man, the increase of plant, the colossal advertisement campaigns, the new buildings, and the carefully spent funds in political propaganda against any rise in the cost of food and other products. This extends even to the placing of candidates for Parliament.

These are world causes of British agricultural depression. Government action in itself has been a potent cause in producing an agricultural depression far deeper than it would otherwise have been. It is the old story of producing a palliative to hide the fundamental evil, and so in effect aggravating it. A conscientious estate owner has now to keep one clerk and a redoubtable nervous system in order to cope with Government forms and inspectors alone. Whenever he builds a necessary cottage he has to get plans passed in triplicate on an unusual map scale by town planning, rural district, and county authorities. Every farmer has to fill in countless forms, and, as ignorance of law is no excuse, he is constantly in hot water. Rural education has been made less effective in rural bias but far more costly by the Hadow System of Central Schools.

The Milk and Dairy Order has made cowshed costs fantastic at the instance of theorists in the Ministry of Health. The scale of rooms and air space per person now enforced for country cottages is planned for an airless town and makes it nearly impossible to house a good workman with a large family. Rates go up to put out-of-door gipsies in new council houses, which they ruin and where they languish. The feckless and the unfit are better treated than any healthy labourer could hope to be, and the bad employer and the speculator are never penalized like the good employer and good landowner.

Thus, without hesitation, one can say that from Land's End to John o' Groats the soil in general is deteriorating. Its best servants among the labourers are disappearing and the ancient skill is being lost. The disappearance of the arable sheep has meant the disappearance of the hurdle-maker, who lost his market for barrel hoops at the same time. This has meant the ruin of the old oak and coppice system of woodland. Insecurity for the future and charges on the land have prevented any high-forest campaign of hardwood planting to replace it. Labour costs have prevented hedgerows from being trimmed; and the jungle, many yards wide, has crept out from the hedges. The same reason has allowed the drains to fall into disrepair, and so rushes and reeds and coarse grass have taken the place of fine grazing. The 'drowner' is seen no more on the water-meadow which has become a snipe bog.

The decline of arable sheep-keeping has meant bad farming in many districts, so that artificial manure and casual fallowing have taken the place of the golden hoof and intensive hand hoeing. There has been a reduction in sixty years of over five and half million sheep. But this does not show anything like the relative loss of sheep population on arable land. In the first place, sixty years ago few lambs were slaughtered and most sheep were killed as prime wethers. In December the sheep census for England and Wales is only about 12,000,000 to-day, while it is about 16,500,000 in June; thus many more than 4,000,000 sheep are slaughtered every year as lambs, and are only on the land for a few months.[1] In the second place, there has been an increase in sheep for grazing in the course of years, especially in the arable areas. This has meant the loss of good arable sheep farming in exchange for indifferent sheep ranching. Even so, there is loss of more than two-thirds in sheep population in East Anglia in three generations of men. The population of sheep in the Home Counties and Wessex

[1] In sixty years the number of lambs reared has declined by 6 per cent., while the number of sheep kept has declined by about 25 per cent. in England and Wales.

has been halved in the same period.[1] The numbers among Down breeds kept purely for arable purposes have probably been reduced by four-fifths to three-quarters. This is the most serious single prospect in the degeneration of good arable farming.

This does not complete the picture of loss of organic manure in the arable counties. The number of beef cattle fattened in yards until very recently has steadily declined, and so the manure cart has disappeared together with the golden hoof. The decline in horses kept on the farm has likewise been enormous. Even since 1914 the decline has been over half a million, or about 40 per cent. of the 1914 horse population on the land. When we remember also that the Army has been almost entirely mechanized, and that in towns the horse for transport is almost an anachronism, we can see that the loss of manure is far greater even than the loss of half a million horses from the farms would suggest.

Now at the same time there has been an increase in the greedy feeding crops, such as sugar-beet and cabbages and kale for human, rather than animal, consumption of over half a million acres. This has meant an enormous total loss of organic plant food which has mostly been replaced by inorganic minerals. These last, whatever their virtues, are effective generally in destroying the soil bacteria, which keeps land healthy and

[1] See *Ministry of Agriculture Statistics*, vol. lxx, Part 1, 1935, pp. 32–37.

provides it with humus. So we see an enormous increase in crop and animal disease which wastes millions of pounds annually. It, moreover, affects crops adversely both as regards quantity as well as quality, and affects the value of such foods for human consumption in a way that has not yet been investigated.

The sum total of this deterioration is cumulative and increases ever more rapidly. Grass as well as crops and animal health has suffered. The dock and thistle, coltsfoot and corn-cockle are the visible signs among the scrannel crops we grow. Docks and thistles blow from the grassland likewise, and in the last five years the poisonous ragwort has become a national menace in the pastures, where thorns and reeds are turning good grass into rough grazing. The land 'walks' hard and without spring as it should do. There are few worms in the soil. Abortion and Johne's disease as well as foot-and-mouth are rife among herds. There is hardly a large flock of chickens free from disease in the whole country. Twenty years ago potatoes were sprayed with copper-sulphate mixtures once or perhaps twice in a year, now they are sprayed twelve or fifteen times a season in the great potato areas. Nearly all of this is due to loss of organic manure for the land and a proper balance of farming. The story is the same with fruit trees and other crops. So it is clear that if we are to have a healthy agriculture we must return to and improve on the practice of our ancestors.

CHAPTER VIII
THE DRY BONES CAN LIVE

THE last chapter showed the dismal picture of our own agriculture which is parallel in many ways to the agriculture of all non-peasant countries, and in a less degree even to peasant countries, which have had to exploit their land to pay debts and taxes.

But there is a reverse side to the medal. We have no dust bowl, our land has a capacity for fertility as good as that of any in the world, and our well-distributed rainfall and equable climate is unsurpassed for agriculture, even though we lie far north for winter sunshine.

In England and Wales we could carry some 10,000,000 cattle without undue strain on the fifteen and a half million acres of grass, since well over two million acres of arable land is under clover and rotation lays, and most of the five million and more extra acres of rough grazing can carry store cattle. But this will involve a temporary increase of imported feeding stuffs until our own land has increased in fertility. Cattle in increasing numbers on the rough grazing would help land that is now overbalanced by sheep grazing only.

The falling off in the horse population alone

allows a considerable increase in summer grazing for cattle; also it means more available hay and oats in winter. We could then be entirely self-supporting in milk production for butter and cheese. This would have the effect of making skim milk available to the extent of well over one thousand million gallons. This would not only make calf-rearing easier and cheaper, but would place our pig production on a balanced and healthy basis, and save over a million tons of imported feeding stuffs. Whole milk sold off the land is a dead loss to agriculture of all its contents, but butter and cheese leave in the skim milk the most valuable organic minerals, while they still supply adult human beings with some of their most-needed fats and most digestible proteins. Thus it is madness from the point of view of a balanced agriculture and national security to discourage milk production except for liquid consumption. A plentiful supply of skim milk would go very far towards eliminating disease from the nation's herds of pigs.

With very little inroads into the land necessary for crop production or the grass keep of other stock, we could be self-supporting in pigs. The pig, when used wisely on grass, is one of the best regenerators of land it is possible to find, and his manure either from the fattening shed or dropped direct on clover and root crops, is extremely rich.

In the Middle Ages the oak and hardwood forest and coppice of England were the accepted grazing-grounds of the swine. A judicious exploitation of our oak and hardwood[1] coppice by pigs would improve the forests and the store pigs alike, as the pig is a woodland animal. Bracken roots, acorn, and beechmast make a delicious flavour in ham and pork, We could at once tickle the palate and save imports of feeding-stuff. The value of a well-established system of woodland husbandry for pigs would be incalculable in war time.

Pig and cow manure is intimately bound up with the fertility of arable and pasture alike. In fact, the more cattle and pigs we have the more will land be reclaimed by the plough to feed them. But if this is true of these animals it is even more true of arable sheep. As extensive grazers sheep are not very good for grass land unless they are balanced carefully with other grazing stock. But both mechanically and organically they are the finest possible improvers of ordinary light and medium arable land. Thus, without seriously impinging on our grass land we could double our sheep population.[2] When we had twenty-two million sheep and lambs in this country seventy years ago, we still had only 6½ per cent. more lambs than we have to-day.

The fact of slaughtering a lamb at an average

[1] The pig destroys most conifers and should not be put among softwoods.

[2] That this, in the summer census, since by January most of the lambs would be slaughtered and only the breeding flocks left.

age of six or seven months instead of at two to three years old, makes it possible to have far larger breeding flocks for production. We could double our present production of lambs and mutton, which would make us self-supporting in war time. But it would have many more benefits than the immediate benefit to arable agriculture, and to employment and security. The first benefit would be to double our home supply of wool and to quadruple our supply of better-class short wools, which means less need to import wool, and less need to rely almost entirely on overseas supplies for clothing. The same applies to the skins and hides of sheep, cattle and pigs. The leather imports, both raw and manufactured, could be reduced. All the by-products in slaughtering would be available without importation, such as canned beef and beef extracts. The land itself would gain enormously from the increased supply of blood and bone fertilizers as well as meat meal for feeding. These organic manures with a high percentage of valuable phosphates and other minerals are safer for the land than artificial manures. These would be available in war when artificial manures would generally be needed for destructive purposes. The land gains nothing when animals are slaughtered abroad for import to Great Britain.

Poultry is the remaining organic fertilizer for the land. As with pigs, so with poultry, we could be self-supporting in about the same time as it takes to build a battleship. But as a matter of policy we should delay doing this until our land is healthier. Healthy land and healthy home-grown food is a necessity to keep flocks clear of disease. We should not, then, run the risk of losses from the diseases which are at present ruining our poultry flocks. Lately poultry farmers have over-specialized, and their feeding has been forced for egg production.

In actual production for human food we would probably return to 12,000,000 acres of arable land instead of 9,000,000-odd now cultivated in England and Wales. Wheat should not be grown as a general policy anywhere more than once in four years; there are probably not much more than 10,000,000 arable acres suitable for wheat in Great Britain, and therefore we should grow about 2,000,000 acres of wheat per annum. This should produce anything from 1,600,000 to 2,000,000 tons, according to the season. In general, we shall increase our arable output with proper farming and organic manure to 50 per cent. above our present output, and still have a large margin of improvement in hand. The increase will not come from spectacular yields, but by good farming with organic manure, which will greatly decrease the number of failures which now reduce the general average per acre. If in an ordinary season the poor yields of wheat were over thirty bushels per acre, then the average production would probably be about forty bushels. This, together with the increase in arable land, should make us capable of a

50 per cent. all-round increase in cereal crop production. It would also go a long way towards reducing the imports of animal feeding-stuffs, as well as the imports of milling wheat.

A steady sugar-beet policy ought to yield an average of half a million tons of refined sugar— enough to supply us with all the sugar essential in war time—even if it is only about one-fifth of what we import and manufacture now.

We ought never to have less than 500,000 acres in potatoes in England and Wales, and with a return to organic manures we should never produce less—including as well allotments and private gardens—than 4,000,000 tons per annum. This would allow a substantial surplus of potatoes for stock feeding, or for producing potato flour for human use, and alcohol for fuel.

Thus we could look forward to a useful increase in the wheat supply already augmented by the quota system in the last few years, and a surplus of potatoes which, in the ordinary course, would save animal food or else save some of the present imports of potato flour.

By an increase in the average acreage of oats and barley in the arable area and by better farming at least 3,000,000 tons for animal feeding, oatmeal and malting barley should be produced south of the Tweed. This is an increase of over a million tons in present average production. In 1935 about a quarter of a million acres were grown of mixed corn, rye, beans and peas, in England and Wales, exclusive of beans and peas for canning and fresh vegetables. This is an acreage that should be doubled and which would be most valuable for stock.

At present there are in England and Wales about only 650,000 acres (exclusive of private gardens and allotments), devoted to vegetables and fruit for human consumption; there is still plenty of room to feed our people entirely on home-grown vegetables and fruit, save for exotic produce out of season. But to do this increased livestock for organic manure is absolutely necessary if disease is to be avoided and steady yields produced from year to year.

The result of such a moderate policy, which would merely set the best form of traditional farming on its feet, would save us from importing all dairy produce and from importing most of our beef and mutton. In war time it would make us completely independent of these imports. It would also save us all pig imports. The total effect of this on employment would be to provide one million people with work on the land and in ancillary industries.[1]

The writer has deliberately omitted Scottish figures of acreage and production. Wheat and sugar-beet acreage are negligible in Scotland. But for the rest Scottish arable farming is still so sound that there will be little noticeable increase for some

[1] See the author's detailed figures and reasons in *Horn, Hoof, and Corn*, published 1932, Faber and Faber.

years. This is not to say that a more fair return for food sold off the land is not needed in Scotland. It is. But the Scottish system of farming is more self-contained, even to the home consumption of home-grown oatmeal. The greatest room for improvement in Scotland lies in the reclamation of rough grazing and the improvement of poor pasture.

It may be said that it cannot be done and has never been done in England. The answer is that until 1860 Great Britain never had any need fully to expand her agricultural production. From Saxon times until the nineteenth century our own pressure of population never made it necessary to use all our land or to farm intensively. In fact we were often exporters of corn to the Continent. The repeal of the Corn Laws followed by the exploitation of the virgin lands abroad in the late 'seventies very quickly suppressed the expansion of good farming at home. Even so, in the early 'seventies we were feeding a much larger human population from home-grown produce and at the same time carrying an equivalent weight of cattle and sheep and horses, without much import of animal foodstuffs or mineral fertilizers. Exploitation of the homeland then started gradually so as to compete with the exploitation of virgin lands abroad.

We have therefore no historical criterion in Great Britain of what we could do, and very little in Europe on a large scale. Germany is our one example; for in 1914 on poorer average soil and with a worse rainfall she produced more per acre than we did. While this was partly the result of good farming, it was due more especially to her pioneering work as the protagonist of artificial fertilizers. The appalling result of this showed in 1914–18 when a large part of her population starved in spite of her being able on paper to produce 85 per cent. of her total food requirements. War cut off or deviated her supplies of mineral fertilizers. In spite of being in 1914 the best-fed nation (including Great Britain) in Europe, she starved because the land without artificial fertilizers failed to keep up her crop production. Her livestock decreased in numbers and there was no reserve of fertility. This could not have happened if she had farmed her land more organically and not over-stimulated it by artificial means. As soon as the pills were cut off constipation of the soil set in.[1] If we were to return to good and only semi-intensive organically manured agriculture we would be saved from that disaster, and we would be independent of artificial aids in future crises.

But if we wish to consider the possibilities of soil production which this island might achieve we must look to the Orient. For some thousands of years China, Korea and Japan have sustained a vigorous and teeming population on a scale undreamed of in Europe. Anyone wishing to study

[1] See Report on food conditions in Germany (Cmd. 280), 1919.

this should read *Farmers of Forty Centuries*, by
F. H. King, a book which should have made all
western doctors and biological scientists rethink
and revalue everything they ever thought and
dreamt.

Japan is an archipelago not unlike the British
Isles in latitude and situation. It is much more
mountainous and difficult to farm. It is without
many of our geological advantages, but it is a
country comparable in its ocean position to our
own. On some 23,000,000 acres—far less than our
own cultivable acres—she nevertheless in 1911
supported[1] over 50,000,00 people. The Japanese
is a byword for bravery and endurance. He is also
quick and intelligent, so we have no advantage to
claim in these respects. In spite of tuberculosis his
bill of real health in far worse apparent living conditions is probably better than our own. There is
only one answer to this—his treatment of the soil
and his use of the sea. There is no room for luxury
or, indeed, anything but the closest economy, but
he does live and thrive where we cannot. Not only
does he produce food in four times the quantity
that we do, but he provides by-products in silk
and other things off the land far in excess of Great
Britain. This is an agriculture carried on with
little or no livestock, but until recently without
any artificial manure. Human beings in Japan are
the equivalent of livestock as producers of organic
fertilizer. And until we use our own night-soil

[1] See *Farmers of Forty Centuries*, by F. H. King.

138

instead of wasting it, we must rely on livestock. In any case, it would be our proper use of livestock that could give us a standard of health and living far above the Japanese. If we use our land and the sea to feed us properly, the products of milk, cereals, vegetables, fruit, together with *some* meat and fish, eggs and poultry, we should be the healthiest nation in the world. Cancer, tuberculosis, constipation, and general morbidity should disappear almost entirely—save among the congenitally unfit and the deliberate misusers of their bodies. Other aspects of Oriental farming will be dealt with in the following chapter, but the fact remains that if we use Japan as a criterion, we should be able to produce double our present quantity of foodstuffs and yet be only half as productive as we could be on such a traditional basis of farming.

This chapter has shown that we have enough land to increase our cattle population by 60 per cent., our sheep and pig and poultry population by 100 per cent., and in consequence, our wheat production by 20 to 50 per cent., and make ourselves self-contained with supplies of vegetables and fruit for everybody in sufficient quantities. Much of this could be done in two years, all of it in ten years.[1] It would save us in

[1] But to accomplish this the mechanical as well as organic regeneration of the land must take place through good fences and by proper drainage of water-logged soils, and a comprehensive water supply for stock.

war time the need to use any shipping or any
Navy in guarding all our most perishable foodstuffs. But in the meantime, if we had one year's
reserve in human and animal foodstuffs, it would
make us not only well fed but independent of all
food supplies for two years at least of war. It
would save us a peace-time bill for more than half
our net imports of food. Above all, it would give
us health.

What have we to lose? Some shipping trade,
some international dividends and some displace-
ment of usurers' trade. The gainers will be
1,500,000 unemployed and those who fear war,
those who hate ill health, those who want security,
and those who love life. Who are the obstacles?
Those, who in the language of the democracy fool
most of the people all the time, who engineer dear
food slogans and thereby manipulate the politicians; those who believe that purse-strings can
bind the world, and who forget that the rare
moments of progress and the few enduring civi-
lizations have happened in spite and not because
of money power.

CHAPTER IX.

REVALUATION

IN the last chapter we assessed only the very moderate possibilities of agricultural production in Great Britain. Some European nations make far greater effort now. But this cannot happen without a change of purpose, or rather a change to purpose from none. This in turn will not happen without a revaluation of all our ideas of life and health and finance.

The purpose of a nation should be vigour and health; and these should endure and grow so that a nation's culture and empire will continue to the benefit of all who are worthy within its borders, not for a few years but many generations. Such being the case, we must revalue everything by the criterion of whether it promotes health now and sound human stock for the future. We have seen how international finance interferes with national regeneration, but there is another form of danger which we must consider in our revaluation. The ordinary man who sees the many millions of people in urban life, who have to be supported by industry, is quite sincere in saying that the cheaper we get our food the better it will be for our people, even if that food is subsidized by our competitors.

On the face of it he is quite reasonable. But there are fundamental fallacies in this. In the first place, we have seen that this leaves us defenceless in war, since our home agriculture will be lost to us by neglect. If it is necessary to be well armed to avoid war, so it must be necessary to be safely fed. It is two aspects of the same problem, and, while we are an empire, neglected land in England is an invitation to others to attack us for our lands abroad. While we are defenceless there can be no national health and no regeneration for the future. But taking an even longer view, we have seen from a previous chapter how exploitation of land is narrowing the world's acres, and that our land in peace time will be needed before long to make up for the deserts elsewhere. Cheap food now may mean famine later.

Secondly, the interest due from the Argentine on our money invested there makes it necessary for the Argentine to sell us about £25,000,000 worth of goods for which we sell them nothing in exchange. If they made a level exchange of goods and services with our people instead of selling us double what they buy from us, we could not be paid interest for our investments. Thus in order to get dividends from foreign investments we draw on moral capital and physical stamina by keeping men out of work. No amount of cheap food can make up for loss of work.

The only healthy trade there can be is an honest exchange of goods for other goods. The same applies not only to food but to industry. Investments which we have made in Japan, for example, put our Lancashire cotton operatives on the dole. Foreign debts alone cause our agricultural home market to be flooded. In other cases, we have acknowledged the principle of how damaging a free market can be to unemployment by a tariff policy, but not so in agriculture, where the damage is worst and the chances of re-employment are highest.

Thirdly, because we are the only free agricultural market in the world every nation with a surplus of agricultural production is bound to try every means in its power of selling perishable produce here. A wit once wrote that polygamy is as natural as having several teacups and one teapot and polyandry is as unreasonable as having several teapots and one cup. In the market for food in Britain the teacup is small but the teapots many.

Thus we have subsidies for agriculture in nearly every nation that competes with our farmers. It is impossible to estimate the total extent and quantity of these subsidies. In order not to burden the reader with unnecessary detail there is an appendix giving certain instances of subsidy by foreign nations to their exports of food stuffs. Suffice it to show the types that exist and something of their widespread nature. The first is a direct subsidy on the product to be sold. Australia subsidizes her wheat, for instance, by a bounty on each acre grown. Some Baltic countries subsidize bacon;

then in this class there is the export subsidy which is very widely distributed over the world. The Germans did this some years ago, to meet reparations and other costs at certain seasons. The French have done it. The next and most potent form of subsidy is to provide an export bounty by a deliberate depreciation of the exchange. Australia and New Zealand do this to the British market and give their producers a 20 per cent. bonus on exports, and by the same token a 20 per cent. protection on imports, so that it works against our farmers on imports and against our industry on exports to those countries. No British workman gains from that. The Argentine also has a manipulated double exchange on their currency which has the same kind of effect, and the Scandinavian countries have linked their exchange to the pound.

Then there is dumping which is not strictly a subsidy but has the same effect. For instance, butter in New Zealand is at times about 50 per cent. more expensive to her own consumers than is New Zealand butter in England. By having to pay more for butter at home they subsidize exports. The New Zealander can buy less from our industrial workpeople, while by securing less for his butter the English countryman can likewise buy less from the English townsman, and so unemployment mounts. In a far more serious way the Russian peasant is incredibly depressed in standard of life in order that the U.S.S.R. Government can dump agricultural products abroad and so pay for foreign debt services and finance revolution in the British Empire and elsewhere.

This form of subsidy by selling under cost of production is universal, for when one single country does it every other country must follow suit in the same commodity, since the English cup is so small and the foreign teapots so numerous.

There is another subsidy where the foreign labourer gives his services for lower wages than our own. Holland, the successful rival of our Fenlands, has a fairly happy and prosperous agriculture and well-farmed lands. Ostensibly, her wages and standards of life are as good as our own. But for the same wages as we pay for a fifty-two-hour week, her workmen work fourteen hours a day in summer and nearly ten in winter. Their housing is neat and good, but by English Ministry of Health standards grossly overcrowded. You may see clean-milk diplomas in excellent, sensible cowsheds, which are none the less sheds which could be condemned outright by the bureaucrats, whom we have to obey in England. At the same time the Dutchman often has to pay more for Dutch food in Holland than he would for Dutch food in England, and in Denmark the Dane eats bacon which is below the grading fixed for export.

Every country's farmers are in debt, which is proof of the exploitation of the land the world over. But ours is almost the only country where

K 145

moratoriums and enforced scaling down of principal and interest on agricultural debt has not taken place. In Poland, when things get too bad they still have a pogrom, but with us the only pogrom is of the land itself, coupled with slow torture of those who live upon it.

Then there is the subsidy on transport which is very much greater than most people imagine. Abroad, most railways are State-managed and agricultural transport has first preference. With us we are forced to use the railway without preference, and indeed with extra expense as in the case of pigs sent to the bacon factory, where other means of transport are available. Shipping subsidies are even more striking. Nearly every country—including at last our own—subsidizes shipping, but in some countries where shipping is regarded as outside the rules of ordinary trading but inside the concerns of national naval defence, the subsidies amount to many millions per annum. Italy and the U.S.A. are the great exponents of this policy, which at once harms our defences by reducing our merchant fleet and puts our seamen out of work and our farmers in difficulties. It is cheaper for the Dane to buy middlings from English mills than for our own inland farmers. It is cheaper to ship wheat from the Great Lakes to Hull than to send it by rail from Hampshire to Birmingham. The final touch of insult in all this is when our own industries, railways and farmers have to pay more for our home-produced coal so that we can give an export bonus for coal to the very foreign industries that already compete with us in a subsidized form. In other words, we subsidize both the export of capital abroad and the ruin of our own capital in the soil.[1]

Now, as it has been pointed out, almost any one of these causes is sufficient to depress the price of foodstuffs in Great Britain to below the cost of production—and it has done so. Over long periods there is hardly any common edible commodity in Great Britain that is not sold wholesale at very nearly half its just wholesale price. Wheat is a striking example. Simply because world wheat reserves have been enormously reduced and American harvests are bad, the price was for a while nearly doubled in two years. In other words, as soon as there is no need to dump or subsidize wheat, prices have found their proper level for the producer. Now such impoverishment of the primary producer has produced an international slave market of unemployment and has made usury the master. It has impoverished and not helped our own working classes. Sooner or later food bought too cheaply makes empty larders and idle hands.

[1] It must be admitted that in the last three years farmers on balance throughout the country have done better than since 1929, though there are depressed districts. What matters is that in spite of this the soil is deteriorating. It is only when farmers and their land are doing well that we can be satisfied. Prices must be too low so long as the land deteriorates.

Any sound Englishman who still believes in his race desires its future. He is only bewildered, wrongly fed and led, and without hope because nothing he has learnt or seen since 1900 can give him hope. If we are to give hope and leadership we must rebalance his life, which will come of revaluing it. A country whose workmen are exploited for the parasite classes is unbalanced. Finance and distribution must be the servants of production, not the masters. Production itself must also be balanced. The old free trade conception of every nation specializing in commodities in which it excels has been proved fallacious by mass production, in which nearly every industrial nation can compete. This belief dies hard. A nation is a body politic, and the free traders' conception among nations is equivalent to believing that, among a group of men, one man's stomach will serve for another's mouth, and another's feet and another's ears are all that is necessary for each man's functions. In other words, vital parts of the national body politic should be left to atrophy in order to magnify some other function. A country entirely given over to specialized industry which is based on export cannot have security even in peace.

A nation balanced between town and country and relying mainly for trade within its own borders is stable. Even if we achieve this balance we must still fight for health against all the things such as chlorinated water, bad air, mechanized occupation, lack of sunlight, and the wear and tear of speed and noise in modern life, which makes health so much harder to achieve.

We have seen how impoverished from erosion and bad farming the land of most food-exporting countries has become. For that reason food from a healthy soil is necessary. We could guarantee this in certainty only from Britain. We alone could guarantee a sufficient quantity of really healthy fresh foodstuffs for our own people, because it is the only area in our control. Even this year's reports by the Ministry of Health—always famous for optimism—stresses the need for more fresh milk and vegetables. Milk, vegetables, and bread, will not nourish properly if they do not come from a healthy agriculture. Cows kept in the dark have been proved to give milk far inferior in nourishing qualities to cows kept more naturally. Proper systems of farming can raise the gluten content of bread by 50 per cent. Ten pounds of well-grown vegetables can do the work of thirteen pounds of poorly grown vegetables. The English soil is the best in the world for crops and stock, and it is the only soil over whose methods of tillage we can have control.

Although there is still a whole new world to explore in good farming, we know enough now to understand that the improvement in the quality of our crops has a possibility once undreamed of. A revaluation of our living makes sound home agriculture a necessity for the bodies of our people.

And even with a sound body, conditions of living which induce a dissatisfied and hopeless mind, end in affecting health and stamina. This is where the greatest need for revaluation exists. We have blindly accepted modern industry as part of our lives, and whether we like it or not it is here as so-called progress. Everyone is called on to adjust himself or herself to it, regardless of what the future holds. Because mass production is the order of the day we think in terms of quantity and not quality; and because science has become god, when things go wrong, we think in terms of material substitutes rather than fundamental physical and psychological health. We measure food in calories and not quality; we measure boredom by providing cinemas, recreation grounds and football matches. It is the old story of bread and circuses substituted for a full life.

It is outside the scope of this book to discuss the way of returning to psychological satisfaction through work in industry. But in agriculture we have the one industry where psychological contentment in doing a skilled and living job is not lost. Man's hands are the oldest expression of his nature, not his mind.

When we begin to understand that there is extra craftsman's work on the land for nearly half the number of our unemployed, we can see that the health of the nation will be affected spiritually as well as physically by tending our soil with love and diligence. There will be also more opportunity thus for men to rise in the walk of life in which their knowledge and skill can make them useful. So we can use our reserves of good stock to water the plants of new leadership; at present we waste these reservoirs to flush the human sewers of the nation.

The farmer himself has need of more knowledge than any bank manager. He must understand the cycle of life and possess an empirical instinct for the secret of growth. He must be a judge of soil-mechanics and a doctor of preventive medicine for animal and plant. He must be a weather prophet, a very skilled organizer of work, and a philosopher who can reckon in years against the disasters of days.

The man who labours on the land needs to be fit in body and skilled in hand. He has to have initiative, since, when things go wrong in the field, he can only rely upon himself. He cannot ask an inspector's advice and wait for others to put things right. He has to understand animals and be a better rough mechanic than a garage-hand, for he must know many kinds of machinery. He sees the crop grow from fallow to harvest and knows how long ahead to plan for the following year; he nurtures animals from conception to the market, and unknown to himself the rhythm of existence is in the marrow of his " ancient, sage, sardonic bones ". He is the actor and spectator, too. Those who live by serving the land indirectly are little less skilled in hand or full in living. The men who build and thatch, who shoe horses and weld machinery, who make the many simpler implements of farming work, all these and a countless list of others, are still part of the great company of craftsmen upon whom health and culture depend. A full agriculture is an old value restored for health of mind as well as body, without which the townsman in the end must perish.

CHAPTER X

RECONSTRUCTION

THROUGHOUT the preceding chapters it has become clear that the restoring of agriculture means something more than the mere increase of production to the nation, and that it means more to agriculture than bigger returns. Without care and wisdom in its service, we can do no more than make the soil a vehicle for the false values of the market-place. Thus we must revalue our code of husbandry and use and improve those methods which immemorial experience has proved to stand the test of health for human beings, and for lasting fertility in that origin of life, the crust of earth on which we dwell.

Sir Robert McCarrison, one of the most experienced doctors and research workers in diet alive to-day, has given us the criterion by which to judge our values. He writes in a paper on "Nutrition and Health", read on May 25th, 1937:[1]

---

[1] *Nutrition and Health* (Gabriel Howard Memorial Lecture, 1937), pp. 23, 24, 25, by Sir Robert McCarrison, C.I.E., M.D., D.Sc., LL.D., F.R.C.P. Formerly Director of Nutrition Research in India.

In this country everyone, or nearly everyone, gets enough energy-yielding foods—bread, sugar, fats—and, except the very poorest, enough meat. But many people do not get enough of " the protective foods ", particularly milk, fresh vegetables and wholemeal bread. Their diets are, therefore, incomplete, and incomplete in a direction which results ultimately in disorder of structure or functions of organs or parts of the body, that is in disease. It is as though motor-cars were given enough petrol but not enough of the things—oil and grease, for instance—needed to keep their mechanism in good running order. . . .

In this lecture I have said little or nothing of the calories, mineral salts, proteins, vitamins or other chemical constituents of food about which you may have heard or read. I have done so purposely. . . . What I want you to learn from this lecture is that it is the foodstuffs themselves that matter to you, rather than any chemical ingredient of them; the foodstuffs, which I have mentioned in the list given above.

These, when properly combined in the diet, supply all the food-essentials, known and unknown, discovered and undiscovered, needed for normal nutrition, provided they are produced on soils which are not impoverished. For if they be produced on impoverished soils their quality will be poor and the health of those who eat them—man and his domestic animals—will suffer accordingly. Man is literally created out of the earth, since it is the earth that supplies, through the agency of plants, materials out of which he is made. If, therefore, he is to derive all the benefits which the earth is so ready to yield to him, he must employ his intelligence, his knowledge and his labour in rendering it fit to yield them to him. In this country impoverishment of the soil goes on apace because we take out of it in the form of crops more than we put into it in the form of *animal and other organic manures.*[1]

This impoverishment leads to infertility of the soil and this in its turn, to a whole train of evils; pasture of poor quality; poor quality of the stock raised upon it; poor quality of the foods this stock provides for man— meat, eggs, milk; poor quality of the vegetable foods he raises for himself; and, faulty nutrition with resultant disease of plants, beasts and men. Out of the earth are we and the plants and animals that feed us created and made, and to the earth we must return the things whereof we are made, if it is to yield again foods of a quality suited to our needs. There is in this country, at the present time, no greater need than that by proper care and cultivation of our soil we may make ourselves self-supporting in the health-giving foods, particularly milk, garden vegetables and potatoes. Unfortunately, it would seem that we cannot grow all the wheat we need for bread; but we can at least turn the wheat we do import, as well as the wheat we grow in this country, into wholemeal or lightly milled flour, using the bread made from it instead of the denatured white bread now in almost universal use. There are few greater services that anyone can render to his country and his fellow-men than to devote his or her energies to the cultivation of the soil. The production of these foods in such abundance that they will be within the means of everyone is a task that lies before the younger generation; and I hope that some amongst you who have listened to me to-day, may devote yourselves to it, and adopt one of the greatest of all pro-

---

[1] The italics are mine.

fessions; that of agriculture. Those of you who have the opportunity should take up the cultivation of kitchen gardens or allotments in your spare time. It is a health-giving pastime; health-giving not only on account of the exercise of your bodies, but because of the fresh foods you produce for yourselves and relatives. There can be no doubt that without the greater production, the cheapening and the more even distribution and use of the foodstuffs I have mentioned, our people cannot attain to that perfection of physique which is their birthright. To this end we must all work together for the common good, even as the cells of the body work together for the good of the body as a whole.

These paragraphs have been quoted at length partly because almost every sentence should be engraved in the mind of any statesman, and partly because it proves that a distinguished man of science with lifelong experience in the laboratory and among men, has reached a conclusion as old as the Pentateuch. The soil should be a living thing which breathes and pulsates with life. It is not a lifeless container of minerals. If we treat it as being alive we shall not only grow good crops and stock, but produce nourishing food for men which feeds them well and gives them health. All life is interconnected, and if soil produces diseased and morbid crops, and these in turn produced diseased animals, so will the food therefrom produce diseased human beings. This is not a matter of scientific speculation but of certainty, and yet many doctors and many scientists still think only in terms of quantity. So many calories of food produce so much life energy they say, and therefore, such and such quantities are enough for a man. If that were so they would never have had to reckon on vitamins and find the difference between margarine and butter in supporting life. But there is more in food than the nicely calculated less or more of vitamins, which in themselves have left the calories theory with only half a truth, just as a theory of nutrition which leaves out right breathing of good air and the drinking of good water is only half a truth. But it is the food we eat for our safety and our health with which this book is concerned, and the key to this lies in the soil. We are not wanting in experience of what is proven here, but we are still half in ignorance of the results of modern methods which are often contrary to experience.

There is a modern school of thought which regards the ground as a bowl into which to put the necessary chemical contents, and that given enough water and crops bred for high production, one can produce anything within the limits fixed by their capacity for nitrogen absorption. This is the school of artificial manuring pushed to its logical absurdity. If that had been a right and feasible method, surely after at least six thousand years of known and successful civilization based on agriculture, it would have been adopted many centuries ago? There is little new under the sun, which those who till the soil have not found out in empirical practice. That is the first test which

157

should make us doubt this school. On some scale, at least ever since minerals have been mined, artificial manuring would have been in vogue if it had *permanently* helped agriculture. Lime and wood-ash and soot have been used for generations since they have been proved useful. This is not to say that other forms of artificial manure may not prove to be good, when they are capable of being incorporated organically into the soil. Until then we must practise the tried and assured methods.

On the other hand, we have some positive proof of the dangers of treating plant growth as a chemical mixture that can be corrected at will by placing certain chemical necessities of plant composition in the soil. In India an experiment in feeding rats solely on whole wheat grown with dung compared to whole wheat grown with artificial manures, has shown life and vigour for the rats fed with the dung-grown wheat, and disease and failure in the rats fed with artificially-manured wheat, in spite of cod liver oil administered to correct the morbidity in the latter.

We can go further. Bacteria and earthworms in the soil we know are essential to create humus and the decay of matter that alone can ensure healthy growth thereafter. It is the old fertility cycle of the legends of Adonis and Tammuz: Life, Decay in the soil and new Life again. Now sulphate of ammonia and many other artificial manures are likely to kill the earthworm and bacterial life of the soil, and so one gets ill-nourished plants which are liable to fatal attack by disease and insect pests. Disease, fungus, and insect pests are always with us, but they chiefly affect the unhealthy plant. In order to cure this condition in the plant, men have not sought the reason for the plant's lack of resistance, but have sought to kill the pest. This, while it has preserved the crop for a few years, has aggravated the cause. For we have in the last thirty years introduced a system of soil and plant poisoning unequalled in folly. Even medical science now realizes that to use continuous strong antiseptics retards the cure of a wound, since it destroys the bacteria that heal as well as those which poison; and yet we do this on the land so much that many research stations are almost exclusively concerned to find some new poison 'voodoo' to save increasingly sick plants. Most of the apples we eat are sprayed with arsenic, and some form of poison is used on nearly all grapes and most fruit. We have started to spray poison to kill charlock and weeds on the soil. The result is to cause a dead, unhealthy soil in which no crop can flourish naturally, and to leave traces of poison in and on human food.

Among animals the lethal effects of Johne's disease, abortion, swine fever, foot-and-mouth and a hundred others, are the result of dead soil and bad feeding. That right feeding of soil and animal can make disease negligible has been proved by Sir Albert Howard in India, and Dr. Pfeiffer in Holland, and elsewhere. The vagaries of climate will probably always make disease a risk, but only a minor one. Nothing can quite compensate for lack of sun or continuous wet weather. At present we are on the fringe of knowledge, but it is more than likely that the things that we learn by a wise intellectual outlook and observation will only be the rediscovery of the instinctive knowledge of the ancients. It was our own ancestors who called the earthworm the " ploughs of God ".

Hence, in the chapter which outlined the immediate possibilities of restoring our agriculture, the policy was to take that type of agriculture for which our soil was fitted, and which experience told us was one which worked well for human health. We have no human wastes to put upon the soil, so we must have animal wastes to give us a proper balance between animal and plant organic matter. The nature of our soil and rainfall makes it possible to graze intensively and with good results to a far higher degree than in the prairies of America or in Africa.

It is one thing to state the possibilities even very moderately of production from our own soil. It is another to show how it can be done successfully. Life is a balance of many things, and so we will have to go contrary to the whole tendency of specialization in farming. For instance, to keep poultry exclusively on a small area of ground in many thousand head without using the plough or composting waste is asking for trouble; so too with pigs. But it is better to vary poultry with sheep and cattle and pigs, and, above all, to alternate crops with grazing. It is better also for the crops to mix the manures from these animals and to make the whole into a form of compost with soil and vegetable matter. In other words, we should adapt the approved and tried peasant agriculture of the East and West to our own farming. If we do this we shall find a miraculous increase in the standard of health of crop, of animal and human being. But we shall also find that it is unnecessary to feed so highly to get the same results. The writer has seen a herd of cows, averaging 1100 gallons carrying flesh and in perfect health, which only received a ration of two pounds per head per day of home-grown concentrated food beside their hay and roots. Anyone who eats really well-grown wholemeal bread or wholemeal macaroni will realize he is satisfied and feels well and strong on 30 per cent. less than the ordinary shop-bought city ration of devitalized foods.

Therefore, it is more than likely that a sound home agriculture will, by the quality of its product, reduce our need for overseas foodstuffs for man and animals by far more than the mere increase in home production. A general increase of 15 per cent in wholesale prices for the home farmer would be quite sufficient to see good farming return and good land made. It would solve debt questions and future credit; and if the nourishing quality of home-grown food appreciated by the same percentage, the public could

L   161

get the same nourishment as now at the same cost. This is one of the most salient economic reasons, apart from national health, to regenerate our land.

It is the right purpose of farming to help nature and not to oppose her, which is an all-important consideration in the future of farming in England. With a soil that is very varied and in most cases geologically excellent, and with a climate that normally distributes its rainfall and sunshine over a long season, the quality of the food we produce, as much as the quantity we can produce, could be the greatest asset that any overcrowded land could have.

The rapid increase of livestock will be made much more possible if we use up all our organic waste in making manure, because this will produce extra grass and arable crops for feeding the stock. It would have the stimulating effect of artificial manures without the possible dangerous consequences. At present nearly all the grass and weeds along our roads are allowed to rot; chaff is often burnt together with haulm and straw and small hedge trimmings. This could go into compost as well as shoddy and town refuse, which now amounts to six pounds per household a day in weight. Of course, the five thousand million tins we consume in towns must be separated and all poisonous materials taken out of the refuse. This can be done and is being done in Southwark, as it is being done in places like Calcutta. It would compensate for the loss of horse manure that used to be so valuable for market gardens near the towns. But, like artificial manures, it should be carefully watched lest even in compost heaps certain ingredients, like printer's ink from newspapers, are found to be harmful. It is too much to hope that we could conserve our night-soil until a wiser generation arises, but we must at any rate do what is immediately possible in stopping the appalling waste which now goes on. It is the waste of organic residue, that is one reason that human food is far more expensive than it should be. Poor soil makes poor health, doctors' bills and, in the end, dear food.

It may be objected that this is a question of labour. It is a question of the cost of productive labour against the price paid for unused labour. While we have a million and a half people out of work—in spite of the present boom condition—the question of the cost of labour does not arise. Huge by-passes extravagantly planned and enormous new municipal centres, expensive additions to mental homes, are all work so nearly non-productive that they are a dead loss in assets. Yet few question this. The men who trim the weeds and grass along our main roads are doing negative work, merely causing a little less thistle down and ragwort to blow. But if they made organic manurial food for the soil by composting this waste, they would be adding to the real capital of the land. So it is with the dustmen and the men who serve the destructors and form the dump-heaps of town wastes. While we have so much unproductive labour and so much unused labour, for which a dole is being paid often for the deterioration of mind and body, to talk of the labour cost of good farming is pure cowardice of mind and bankruptcy of purpose. Nowhere does the writer propose to deal with costings and the 'economic' cost of producing crops or livestock. This is a value that comes from the factory and the ledger. It has no reality in agriculture. Apart from the variation in cost caused by weather, each operation on the land means taking out of it or putting into it so much capital, which can only be measured by the effect in one or many years to follow. No man can measure the cost of health or ill health in his body by pounds, shillings and pence. So in agriculture 'costs of production' are no more than a rough guide for good or bad organization.

The same thing applies to the neglect of field drainage and the inability of farmers to keep their land clean of weeds and free of the encroachment of the jungle and their hedgerows. Every penny that is paid in the dole and every penny supplied by State and County for unproductive labour and materials, is an increase in the cost of living, because in the end only production can pay for it.

This end of waste must be made if we are going to have a restored agriculture; only if this is done will healthy food become a reasonably cheap commodity-within reach of all. We can and do compel parents to send their children to school and to drink only at certain times and to live only in certain houses, and in a hundred and one other ways the tyranny of the State is felt. Surely then some form of labour organization for the youth of this country is not impossible, so that every young man and woman of every walk of life could be made for six months or a year to serve his country in some constructive way of manual labour? This would restore discipline and self-respect and prevent the present appalling waste.

Now there is not a purposed balance in values between, say, the wages the Midland bootmaker may earn, who has to buy the cowman's milk, and the wages the cowman receives, who has to use the bootmaker's leather. Rent is far more expensive in relation to pre-war days than food, and so is clothing; the price we pay in taxation for social services again has no relation to the wages of the producer. The cost of transport has no relation to the price of food or the miner's wage. Until there is a balance in the wages of all workmen and of the rewards of the distributor, it is impossible to speak of food being dear, and until there is a balance in standards of life between ourselves and those with whom we trade—not for overseas dividends but for exchange of commodities—we cannot measure the cost of food from abroad. Dear food is no more than a catch cry produced in the interests of international trade.

We can only reckon on the cost of waste to-day and the danger to health, safety and independence in our nation, when we reckon the final cost of leaving our land half derelict as it is.

So we must make a beginning by having no waste in organic matter returned to the soil, for it is what we put into the land that enables us in fairness to the soil to take from it. The soil will only serve us if we treat it reverently as our master.

There is more in methods of regeneration than an accumulation of organic matter, the cleansing of drains and the trimming of hedges. We have seen how livestock should be balanced on the land and crops likewise. But in our treatment of the soil we are only beginning to recover our ancient knowledge. The cultivation of big acreages in a single crop is bad ranching and not good farming. The ancient strip cultivation of the common field was far wiser. As yet we do not know the limit of influence between one crop and another. In all ancient and successful agriculture mono-culture of one crop over a wide area is never prac-tised. The indiscriminate grubbing up of hedges is also a dangerous thing, since hedgerow shrubs penetrate to the subsoil and are of immense value for drainage, natural manuring, and windbreaks. If it had been otherwise, our ancestors would have grubbed them a long time ago; for it is more diffi-cult to turn an ox on the headland than a tractor. We will have to learn that land to be well farmed must have a balance between crop and grass and between field and shrub and woodland.

166

Modern implements if used wisely may be of the greatest benefit, but if used merely to produce cheap food may ruin the land. Huge acreages in one crop—and the writer is not without personal experience—cheap mass cultivation without proper organic manuring, will be disastrous. We owe a great debt to the pioneers of mechanization, like Mr. Dudley of Linkenholt and others, but those of us who have mechanized are still the pupils of nature, as well as of mechanics. Modern machinery has great use in that its speed can give one the chance of sowing and harvesting in tricky weather, but it is dangerous in the temptation it gives to ranch. The Combine Harvester is very useful at times to cut corn cheaply and save threshing costs, yet it is doubtful if the grain so cut is as valuable for baking as grain ripened in the rick for six weeks. The most expensive method in the long run may be the soundest. The purpose of modern machinery should be to do the work of the horse faster and more efficiently. There is now at least one small tractor on the market which can replace the horse in every operation for the small farmer and do the work with much greater speed. This is a far greater advance in modern mechanization than all the great high-powered mass cultivation machines put together. Even so, while time and labour may be saved by such a machine, it must be remembered that there will be a loss of horse manure. Although this may be made up by other animal manure, the midden will have lost

167

an intangible asset in balanced manuring. The value of urine from the entire horse, for instance, is something which every good farmer probably knows, but it is out of all proportion to its analysis in the great bulk of manure used on a farm.[1]

There is another great chance of advancement through crop-drying, but it will be a disaster if it is a specialized form of agriculture and not a part of mixed farming.[2]

The whole of the foregoing pages are an effort to revalue agriculture in the light of what we know has succeeded and what we can now see to be failing. The first lesson to be learnt is that nature is something that we cannot short circuit; and that in face of lost tradition and our immense ignorance still of the workings of life, we still have to use humble observation and previous experience instead of playing ourselves into the arrogant hands of the abstract scientist. Exploitation of the land is producing desert; farming on a large, extensive scale for quick returns is producing desert. Scientific palliations for crop and animal disease are not creating health; but in the case of sprays are poisoning land. Land cannot be filled with inorganic chemical substitutes for healthy organic matter. Such being the case, we must return to

[1] A consideration of the question of research on the interaction of one plant or animal on another may be found in the appendix, page 263.
[2] See pages 260–1.

peasant farming and more individual care in farming for national safety in peace time and war. We cannot allow scientific exploitation of land for temporary economic gain. And so the problem reduces itself to the statesman's purpose, which should be a healthy balance of national life, a conservation of our resources against an imminent rainy day, and a future healthy life for our peoples. To do this there must be a guiding control sufficient to guarantee the pursuit of such purpose and sufficient freedom for individual initiative to work the soil as experience and love of the soil dictate.

"The master's foot is the best dung", but the committee table is as barren as committee-managed land would become. The more individual masters the more intensive will the dung become. This does not mean to say that the land must immediately be parcelled out among smallholders, but that every encouragement for smallholders to grow naturally should be given.

The first and foremost thing in this is to restore to the land the prosperity it has lost by nearly a century of accumulated neglect and taxation.

Food is relatively dear to produce in England because of the cheap food that has ruined the fertility of English land. Tithe has become heaviest on the light arable land because of its original method of imposition at a time when light land was intensively farmed for corn. For a hundred years nearly three million pounds a year of tithe has been taken from the land. For something like

thirty of that hundred years at least two million
pounds a year has been taken as of statutory right
from land which could not pay it except out of
capital or at the expense of necessary upkeep.
Tithe and death duties have therefore removed
over one hundred and thirty million pounds of
necessary upkeep for the land; and the cheap food
policy since 1880 has been responsible for exploiting farming in varying degrees to the tune of
fifteen million pounds a year at least, on the
average, which has forced the industry to make
profits by the neglect of land and labour and
buildings.

The only reason why the land is not now utterly
derelict is because so long as they could, landlords
have invested outside income and capital again and
again to repair the losses of land itself. Perhaps
the most striking commentary on the present result is that in parts of England the capital value
of the tithe is more than the capital value of the
land and buildings on which it is imposed. In
hardly any part of England is the saleable value
of land as much as the replacement value for insurance of the buildings upon it. For those who
like 'economic' politics, this in itself is enough
to refute the stale cry that the land was stolen and
belongs to the people; since if we judge by the
buildings alone, disregarding drainage, roads and
improvements, the land is a minus quantity in
capital value.

The land, therefore, has a right to special pleading that national money be spent on its regeneration.

If the method is right—and there is real protection in any form so that the right kind of farming is made to pay—there will be little difficulty in finding the finance for it, even if interest rates are kept very low under the present system of usury. This in itself will enable smallholdings to grow under the right circumstances. Land settlement without hope for farming is folly. If it is made successful it is made so at the expense of the legitimate farmer and his men, since it provides buildings, improvements, marketing, buying and supervision practically free in competition with the masters and men who have struggled for a generation against adverse conditions. The men who should have first opportunity to become smallholders are those who have served an apprenticeship to the land as farm labourers. Probably the landlord would be the best vehicle for this (if he could secure the necessary capital money) by the methods of the old copy-hold system. Thus he could, in the way of natural growth, give his best men their first opportunity to become independent by financing all their capital in return for a share of their produce. The landlord could thus co-operate in buying and selling, and guide, lead and direct.

The landlord system in some form should go on because, first of all, it is the one way of keeping responsible leadership on the land, and, in the second place, because it is now ingrained as part of English life and has been proved to cause a loss wherever it has lapsed.[1]

It can exist independently with and as father to the yeoman system, which should be the backbone not only of farming but of national life. Death duties on land and likewise on all responsible ownership of property in contra-distinction to money merely invested in stocks and bonds should be abolished. In return, wherever land is irresponsibly administered, it should be subject to sequestration. There would be no absenteeism in that case, and leadership would return to the land instead of stockbrokers' shooting syndicates. Likewise land should be the hardest property to alienate from its responsible owner. Not one generation but many go to the knowledge of each field. Nothing is so precious for the stability of a nation as love and tenacity of a particular piece of land. To treat land as a marketable chattel is to undermine the very foundation of national life.

These are the first points of agricultural policy in a true national purpose, the second will be to ensure no waste, which means the maximum of labour on the land, for only so is good farming possible. We have already shown how dear food is the direct product of waste, so every farm must in the long run try to be self-contained. The pur-

---

[1] Even in 1925 the capital value of farm lands was £815,000,000 (land, buildings, etc.), while tenants' capital was £365,000,000 (stock, machinery, crops, and tillages).

chase of external feeding-stuffs is only temporarily necessary, because the return of livestock to the land is necessary to restore its fertility. When that is done it will be possible to farm far more cheaply, because animals can be fed and land manured with little recourse to outside aids.

Let us take hay-making as an example. Hay from good land well harvested should be able to feed cattle far better than hay from poor land poorly gathered. Hay cut early and made by the age-old method of tripod curing is both fodder and concentrated food in one. But this requires extra hand labour which will be worth it, if the land is in good heart. It could cut the concentrated food ration of milk or beef cattle in half.

Roots are another case. Where there is plenty of dung and compost, artificial manures are not necessary to grow roots. What is even more important in winter rations is that the root clamp is the only really sound means of giving animals organically the mineral requirements for their bodies. This will reduce the veterinary bills and the wastage from disease, which is a very high but often unreckoned cost of the farming. The root brake is vanishing from the rotation now because it is a crop demanding intensive labour.

Again, the right relationship of arable to pasture can only come about when each has been improved. Good pasture by carrying more stock will enable the farmer to plough some of his land now

173

tumbled down to grass. Deterioration of land in this way has been even more serious in the pasture land of the West of England than in the arable counties. Grass fields are wasting and fences neglected everywhere. One of the reasons of this is that to economize in labour the old arable fields on these farms have not been cultivated and the remainder have been ranched. Much pasture that was once highly productive is now rough grazing, whether reported as such or not. Artificial manures and bought concentrated foods have taken the place of the dung heap, the oatfield and root brake. A well-stocked farm and an increased root and oat acreage would mean that, save for extra labour, there would be no expenses for bought foods and manures. The old high protein analyses recommended for animal feeding are as nothing in comparison to the quality of the food consumed, and the best quality comes from the best-managed land.[1]

The same thing applies to the great arable areas of East and South. If there were enough pigs and yarded bullocks and enough arable sheep, the potato, sugar-beet and wheat grower could cut down his bills for artificial manures, poison sprays, feeding stuffs, and his losses from disease in crops as well. In 1870 we carried a much larger head of sheep

[1] When land is neglected for two or three years because low prices make it impossible to employ enough labour, it gets beyond the farmer to put it right, and deterioration once started becomes a snowball.

and bullocks in this country. Yet we used little or no artificial manures, much less imported food-stuffs for animals, while our crop production was the highest per acre among the western countries.

We can see the reverse of this in the operation of the Potato Board and the Wheat Act. The Potato Board simply limited acreage without regard to methods of farming, and kept their prices up in glut seasons by using the riddle which only allowed the larger potato to be marketed, while at the same time the use of pigs to eat the small potatoes was not profitable. By an arbitrary limitation of acreage to existing growers, those farmers who were already growing too large a proportion of potatoes on the land were allowed to continue, and those who might well for the good of their land have started to grow a small acreage, were debarred except after payment of a high fine. Too large an acreage of potatoes in relation to the size of the farm means bad farming and exploitation of land for quick returns. A proper limitation of national potato acreage might have restricted, however unpopular it would be, the area under potato crop on any farm—for example, to five-sixteenths of the rotation and have allowed any new grower to come into production. A proper cure for potato gluts in a heavy cropping year would have been either the encouragement of pigs to consume a fixed quantity or a series of farina or alcohol factories on the lines of sugar-beet factories. The fact that all potatoes have to be oversized for sale in glut seasons means that the public are deprived of the best quality of potatoes for food value. In order to get large potatoes the potato-grower has recourse to very heavy dressings of artificial manure, which again exploits the land. This, in conjunction with a sometimes too large potato acreage in his rotation, has increased potato diseases and the use of poison sprays.

The Wheat Act has not been an Act of limitation, but of limited expansion. If the Wheat Act had been part of a great general purpose to regenerate agriculture, it would have been excellent. It still is a somewhat faulty model of what should be done in happier circumstances. Standing as one isolated Act, it has led to the growing of wheat on some land not best suited to wheat; it has given a premium to the most soil-exhausting cereal crop in a depressed farming rotation. Wheat alone has paid, so wheat has been grown too often on the rotation and with artificial manures, since there was no bounty on the dung heap. Much more wheat might be grown without exploitation than is grown now, but it will only be grown properly, when there is a bounty in some form or other on the dung heap and the sheep fold. Government policy should always be to help good general farming and not to throw lifebelts to odd parts of the industry at moments of submersion. This has been the only policy to date. Throwing the lifebelts has never brought the industry nearer the shore, but has kept certain sections just above water and well

176

out of sight of land. The Government spends its time congratulating itself on being able to throw lifebelts in mid-ocean, while protesting that all is well if the ship of agriculture is barely kept afloat with starting timbers and rotten stays. Otherwise it seems to think it would be too expensive if the ship were well found and well kept. That the crew is short and living among bad and dangerous conditions does not worry the Government. But the purpose and method do matter to the nation if not to the politician and commercial interests.

From this it will be seen that the key to successful farming is self-contained farming that buys little from outside and returns all its waste to the soil, and that specialized farming is a dangerous thing for the land and for the farmer. The only part of farming that can reasonably be specialized is vegetable and fruit farming, and even this succeeds best with a balance of livestock, and only succeeds ultimately in other conditions if large quantities of organic manure and town waste are available. All forms of bought-in supplies add to the complexity of farm economy and the cost of food.

Even in the ordinary mixed farm there is a great extravagance in bought fuel power. In many districts the adjoining woodlands should supply the motive power in the shape of wood waste gases or ·charcoal gas in internal combustion engines, rather than by oil purchased from abroad. The old industry of charcoal-making in hard wood and coppice forests should be revived in modernized form. Sawdust, lop and top from forest trees and undergrowth are to-day practically unsaleable, but these would cheapen the cost of food, if engines were adapted to use them as prime movers on the farm. On the other hand, this would not please international oil interests, whom the manufacturers of engine and machinery have to please. Thus Germany and Italy lead us in the use of home-grown fuels. For the same reason windmill and watermill are alike in disrepair; these things, like the waste of organic refuse and the derelict state of farm land, are the real reason for the relatively high cost of production from the land to-day, as they are for the relatively low production per acre.

Waste from vermin in agriculture is one of our worst troubles. Estimates of damage done by rats vary from fifty to one hundred million pounds a year. Of this it is quite certain that agriculture bears at least 10 per cent. in loss to cereal crops and food stores in barn and granary.

The farmer's wife loses in chicks and eggs, and hedgerows and banks are riddled as well as thatch and the walls and floors of buildings. Rabbits do more field harm than rats because they poison the ground itself and eat the crop as well; though rats and rabbits each devour where they can. Both are pests whose fertility make unremitting and stringent control essential. Pigeons do very serious damage, especially to green crops and young grasses. These plagues are the result of upsetting the balance of nature. It is the port towns which are responsible for most of the rats. But it is the lack of hawks, owls and weasels which makes the unnatural spread of vermin so easy. Nor are these the only vermin. Sparrows, chaffinches, starlings and rooks are useful in limited numbers, but they are a curse when they go unchecked. They are responsible for much loss at seed time and harvest. No one enjoys blood sports more than the writer, but he holds no brief for the type of farming which is conducted merely as an adjunct to sporting amenities, in the hands of the keeper.

The control of vermin cannot be secured unless it be by a general effort, which includes towns as well as country. Rat, rabbit,[1] pigeon, sparrow and mice cause anything from fifteen to twenty-five million pounds worth of loss to the farmer in a year. Once again it is care and human labour that can prevent this loss if we look on farming as a national asset instead of a picturesque anachronism for the urban holiday-maker. A vermin-free land in war time might just make the difference

[1] Experiments in Wiltshire have shown that four rabbits and their increase can reduce the fertility of one-eighth of an acre of pasture to one-eighth of its former value for feeding in fifteen months. This process in varying degrees is taking place all over England owing to bad keepering and the indigence of farmers who can no longer pay for labour to destroy rabbits which have no market value. See *Farmer and Stockbreeder*, August 11th, 1937, p. 1937.

between starvation from waste and enough food for survival.

It may be argued that many things in this chapter are unfamiliar to modern farming practice, and that therefore even if it were policy it is not immediately possible owing to the necessary revision of ideas. Yet nothing that has been written is not part of successful and agelong farming practice in some part of the world, and much of it is in the bones of the old-fashioned farmer and wise old farm labourer. It is still true that the farmer who is fifty years behind the times, and who refuses to cease farming in the ancient ways up till the moment of his bankruptcy, may yet prove to have been the pioneer of the farming in the future. Superficial modern tradition is in the wrong. The deeper instinct is not.

But we have exceptions in the intellectual world who can teach us. Professor Stapledon has revolutionized methods of grassland farming by going back to the plough for grassland. He has taught us that our good pastures are poor in comparison with their possibilities, and that rough grazing can be turned into the equivalent of what is now considered fair cultivated pasture.[1] Sir Albert Howard has restored to us the lost knowledge of how to

---

[1] In comparison with the 25,000,000-odd acres of more intensive farm lands of these islands, rough grazings are a small matter, but they become important as they cease to be rough. They are, moreover, an indication of what could be done with the better land by applying better methods.

convert organic waste into compost cheaply and well. He has been able to show that the problem is not merely one of having organic manure, but of its proper decay into humus. Green manuring, for instance, following his principles which are only a rediscovery, can be used profitably and without failure. Under present practice many a time green manure, ploughed into cold land which is then sown at once, fails in its effect because it has not had a chance of rotting into humus owing to lack of decaying organic residue and soil warmth. Men like Sir Albert and Dr. Pfeiffer have followed the line of investigating health in crop and animal, and so have sought the cause of disease instead of the palliative. Their results have been more important than all the various poison spray discoveries, vaccine injections, and viruses put together, because they have discovered that health and resistance to disease lies in the health of the soil. This is a conclusion at which Sir Robert McCarrison has arrived and others with him from the medical approach through human beings. For instance, the same rice diet in India will produce health in one place and a deficiency disease in another simply from a difference in irrigation of the paddy-fields by running water or stagnant water. When the irrigation is corrected the disease no longer prevails. What matters is that we have the technique with the intellectual knowledge behind it, but more than that it is not a technique that will take years to acquire by the general farmer, because it exists in his heart of hearts; it is a technique that is in the blood of his ancestors. This does not mean that the intellectual technique will not need to be adapted and revised from field to field, but that its general principles hold good. The technique will not be revised in the light of other principles, only by better methods being used to apply these principles from experience and observation.

CHAPTER XI

THE COROLLARIES OF A REGENERATE AGRICULTURE

A T the risk of some repetition it is necessary to summarize the effects of a sound home agriculture on other aspects of national and imperial life. These are examined under the headings which follow.

Labour

The importance of real purpose has been shown. The writer has laid some stress on method, since it is urban governments which now control, and ignorance of agriculture makes it easy for them to pursue a good purpose and achieve another and worse one by divorcing purpose from method. In applying the right method which follows from our purpose, the most striking thing is that the land requires much labour if it is to be kept healthy. In ten years half a million more people can return to the land by producing our requirements of butter, cheese, milk, bacon, pork, and poultry at home and by increasing our beef production by half as much again, and doubling our sheep population, which in turn will increase our wheat, vegetable and fruit production. The more our land becomes fertile the more stock and crops will we grow and the more intensive will our production become until we become practically self-supporting in all—except perhaps wheat, in a good year. In the end the figures of re-employment would be nearer one million than half a million, and the figures of employment in ancillary industries would rise proportionately.

But this pleasant prospect will immediately be questioned by the cry of "Can you get the labour?" Every year for half a century men have left the land, and this year is no exception. Rural distress has made them seek urban work or urban doles. Moreover, their wives have preferred the second-hand fleshpots of the town to the very real difficulties of country life. The very mechanization of mind and physical qualities have put appreciation of the living reality and potential health of agriculture at a discount. Life at second hand is more desirable under present values.

So we find that a problem *has* been created and the well-meaning mediocrities who take second-hand life like the projected glycerine tears of film stars as 'progress' are busy thinking of palliatives. One says "improve rural housing and amenities"; another says "Morris dancing and village cinemas"; another says "Night Schools"; and the prize ass says "Bring the towns closer and make it easier for everyone to have, as it were, an *urbs in rure*". In other words, since town standards are those apparently most valued, they would have us turn the country into the town. It is all very well meaning and is the product of the garden city mind. Light and sanitary dwellings are right and necessary, but these will come automatically and by country and not by town standards if we have a sound agriculture.

The problem is much more fundamental, it is one of statesmanship and courage. First and foremost it is one of balanced values in national life, the values that make cowards of politicians, since these mean having to face truth. Many party men gladly deprecate buying goods made by poorly paid or sweated foreign labour, when this fits in with the home propaganda of big home business interests. The standard of life of the Japanese and the Poles, they say, menaces that of our own people when their respective goods come into competition. They are quite right, but they only apply the moral outside the country and only on behalf of powerful concentrated sections of voters at home. It does not suit them to apply it to agriculture, nor to be ashamed that some industries should have disproportionately high rewards compared to the most skilled and important of all industries, namely agriculture. If there is to be justice, health and safety in national life, then land labour should not be grudged a right reward, even if it means putting up the cost of food so that it may become level with other necessities such as housing and clothes and transport. This applies

likewise to the farmer himself, who, when a small-
holder, is a labourer as well.. If rewards are to be
in proportion to the responsibility, trusteeship and
skill which good landwork requires, then land-
workers deserve a higher than average meed in
national life. By their duties should men be
judged for their privilege.

The problem is one in the second place of restoring right values to the people of the country,
not of bringing false urban values to the land.
Modern education has overlaid the right values
and robbed men of a sense of responsibility; thus
the dole is regarded as a right if there is no work
in the trade in which a man is registered. Moreover, it is almost impossible for men even to work
voluntarily, if they are on the dole, on account of
State regulations based on false conceptions. The
State regulations are the outcome of false values,
the false values have not been made by the State
regulations, but they have grown with the State's
acceptance of them. This will always be the vicious
circle of democratic party government, which is a
competition in State bribery. The first thing
needed is leadership in the teaching of right
values. A good housewife will learn that a cottage
garden near a farmyard with plentiful manure, or
her husband's right to keep and be allowed to
slaughter a pig, means a greater saving and advantage in fresh vegetables and health than electric
light and tramways do in amenities. With a full
and exuberant country life cinemas and football

matches (amusement as looking on and not as act-
ing) will no longer be considered necessities; and
the merry England, which knew none of these
things, will return. In a sound agriculture the
unhurried cycle of the soil and the full life of
skill and the opportunites for real housekeeping
will attract those who have had their fill of the
noise, restlessness and rootlessness of towns. So it
is a question of re-education and leadership; it has
happened in Germany and Italy in a very few
years, but not by the compulsion of dictators but by
leadership towards the realization of sound values
after too much experience of corrupt values. It is
even more a problem for the women than the men.

After revaluation we could infuse true health
into our teaching by making education something to restore sound instinct and tradition rather
than a school of examinations in potted information, or irrelevant ill-digested book learning. We
should not need physical training grants and the
paraphernalia of gymnasia if the foundation of
health in body and mind were right. We would
not have to teach craftsmanship by classes in fret-
work.

Irish labour is imported for the harvest when
we have a million idle men in England.
Colossal road scheme and aerodrome levelling are
done in argricultural areas by removing men
off the land, while there is a real dearth of
labour now in agriculture. Yet there are over a
million idle men in industry and few think it

wrong to continue to take the dole, even if work in other trades is offered. But their fellow-workers pay for it.

The whole system of compulsory as opposed to voluntary insurance is probably wrong. But even so, if the Government merely had the courage it could lead by saying that only skilled workers who had passed through a sound apprenticeship would be eligible for the dole if they refused to work in other trades. Men would then realize that they had responsibility. It is right that the skilled worker who has fitted himself for one particular job should have the opportunity to wait for an opening in his own trade. It is wrong in general that a bricklayer's mate who has left the land to help on a public building for a few weeks in an unskilled capacity should be entitled to the dole on refusing a job in any other industry than building.

The restoration of agriculture would then absorb in a few years nearly everyone unemployed in Great Britain except the unemployable. Every workman would gain in security and in pocket, as it would no longer be necessary to have high rates of contribution for unemployment insurance; the gain would be greater, since employers would have less to pay in contributions and also in taxation, which in itself would cheapen the cost of living. Moreover, apprenticeship in trade would be helped by the acknowledgment of the skilled worker's status and his due in extra privilege.

But to some extent the future supply of agricultural labour is in the farmer's hands. He too must have the right values. He it is who can bring unity to his own industry by standing first and foremost for his men. It is his business to create public opinion among his fellow-farmers against the black sheep, who exploits his men, and who cares for profits to the exclusion of his men's welfare. Agriculture is still not a limited company; it is still not part of a soulless big business amalgamation, and we should be thankful that it can never be. Agriculture can therefore give the lead, since it has never quite lost it, in responsibility for the welfare of its workers. The State is trying by every means in its power to destroy this. But farmers can still prevent this; and they can see to it that in the country at least the healthy and intelligent boys can have a brighter hope in living on the land than in any tinsel lures the town can offer.

The Breeding of Man, Crop, and Livestock

The soil is the control, as it were, in fecundity. We have seen in agriculture in the last two decades unexampled efforts to produce more without extra expense. The emphasis has been on increased returns with no more effort on the soil. Milk cows have been forced by feeding of concentrates to yield results for which they are not constitutionally capable. Wheat varieties have been introduced with greater yields, but no more humus in the soil; egg production in poultry has been stimulated likewise by artificial methods and artificial lighting. So the story runs with other crops and fruit and livestock. The result is only a fevered research on new viruses and new poisons for pests to check the losses. No one believes more than the writer in blood and the value of genuine pedigree. Careful breeding and selection will produce plants and animals capable constitutionally of giving high results. But there is the limiting factor which we must recognize. Environment cannot easily destroy the inherited capacities of plant, animal, or man, yet by it they can be neutralized. Forced production in bad environment of soil and soil-feeding can go further and destroy by disease, for there is no lasting constitution where there is no chance of health to resist disease. Thus we are utterly unable to judge the capabilities of improvement in man, animal, or plant until the soil itself is made the best possible one in and on which to breed.

Once we have brought back fertility and health to the soil, breeding can come into its own, but not before. Unless we have the essential of a healthy agriculture all production will be forced and end in death.

Most important of all is the effect on man himself. Throughout this book there has been insistence on health and how health comes from the soil. It is the right care of our soil that can restore fecundity to our national stocks; fecundity with health. Our northern stocks flourish best of all away from cities, we cannot preserve our type if our agriculture is derelict, but if it is healthy we can breed the men and women who will be acceptable to people the new lands and tip the scales from corruption and decay to fullness of life at home.

Security

The labour question was put first because it is more important. It is the fundamental point of security together with sound breeding.

We have seen that the first thing for immediate security is a food reserve for animal and man. But it is only a makeshift for immediate needs. The right use of the land will mean, above all, increased health, which is vital for defence, even if it cannot be measured in statistics. The second result means the gradual ability to lessen the necessity of large food reserves; and even more— to make us entirely free of need to import food in a long struggle. The third result is to produce a class of man who will be invaluable in the fighting Services as this class has always been. Men who are skilled in many ways and able to adapt their craftsmanship are especially important in a machine age. The agricultural labourer to-day must be a general mechanic and craftsman.

Another result will be to have much more of

the raw material for boots and clothing available as we increase our cattle by over 3,000,000 head and double our sheep population. There is always a shortage of these necessities in war time. In the same connection a restored agriculture will enable mechanized transport to be more easily available in war. The firms, especially tractor firms, who make agricultural machinery will be equipped for mass production of roadless transport. The tractor, and probably the caterpillar, whatever its abuses in agriculture, has come to stay. Therefore, the Government should, for military purposes, finance a light caterpillar for agriculture which will be equally valuable for transport of men and light artillery. Just as the Government used to rely on agriculture for its draft horse reserve, so it should rely on agriculture for its mechanized tractor reserve. Moreover, if there is any return to cavalry, agriculture is always there to supply a reserve of horses and men as before.

The final consideration is important beyond anything else, if we envisage, as we must, the possibility of defeat. Aeroplanes might just possibly wipe out cities, and war can spread fire and disaster and famine. There are always these possibilities, as there is always a chance of military defeat. If that happened we would need as large and as healthy a population as possible on the land where aeroplanes and famine will not come. In such a case, out of adversity the nation could regrow itself by the seed of its best survivors. If we face defeat with the countryside depopulated as it is now, we should have little hope indeed of rising from the ashes.

The Price of Food

It became clear in the corollary dealing with labour that a balance of life was necessary to secure just rewards for all producers and especially for those concerned in agriculture—the most skilled, responsible and vital of all industries. We could not shrink fiom the fact that the cost of food might justly have to advance to a level with other necessities of life, but the very fact of a properly cared for soil at home will have far-reaching consequences on the cheapness of the production of food at home. The cost of food comes from human labour, from the capital cost of buildings and machinery and things bought off the farm. These are the points wherein a national balance must be struck. But the cost of food is also vitally affected by waste, which comes from neglect. The first reduction in food costs should come from a proper education for our womenfolk. There is scarcely a household account that is not 25 per cent. too large because of the wasteful use and choice of food. If all the food advertisement campaigns were concentrated on teaching a balanced ration for necessities there would at once be a great saving. "Eat more fish", "more fruit", "bread for energy," milk publicity, and all the patent foods are each competing with advertisements in a fantastic hyperbole of claims. But a proper teaching of balanced meals and food and household economy would secure results happy for everyone at home except the distributor, since he would have less to distribute.

In schools and clinics all the hygienic campaigns in the world would not be so valuable as the teaching of good cooking and good housekeeping.

But the economics of the soil itself would cheapen the housewife's budget. First we have seen how the quality of a healthy soil will make it necessary to eat less when food is well grown. This in itself could pay for the extra labour on the soil and the extra rewards for that labour. It is not only the saving in bills for food we should get, it is the saving in doctors' and dentists' bills and in time off for illness and better work through health. Much more than half the time off caused by the colds, bad teeth, tuberculosis, and general morbidity could be saved if we ate wisely on healthily grown food. But if that is true of doctors' bills it is true of veterinary bills and poison sprays. A farmer's risks—apart from the weather and the loss caused by weather and weather-bred disease—should be almost nothing. As it is, disease of animals alone probably costs £15,000,000 per annum, but we have yet to learn the full savings to be effected by animals in first-rate health. The disease we can recognize is as nothing to the loss caused by the half-health in livestock with which we often have to be satisfied. For it is not only human beings who can flourish on a smaller ration of healthily grown food, it is animals as well. If abortion, tuberculosis, swine fever, foot-and-mouth, Johne's disease, and the many ailments of sheep and poultry, were things of small consequence we could have saved very largely. But if because of their health, which resisted these diseases, animals could be more fertile and eat less we should have a new era in farming economy.

The tale of good husbandry does not end there. It is probably unwise to force crop production in general farming beyond a certain point. But if we had nothing save weather to fear for our crops we could produce a far higher average crop of most commodities by having very few failures. We should be saved the poison spray and the harm it does to man and soil alike. Add to this the saving in loss from vermin, such as rats, sparrows, and pigeons, and we have the prospect of low prices with greater rewards in the final adjustment of agriculture. There would be less animal foodstuffs to import, fewer chemists' and veterinary bills on the farm, and a far higher average production. One hundred million a year on new improvements, extra and higher paid labour for the land, might yield fifty millions in saving and a hundred millions in extra production at no higher prices.

Trade

Those who glibly repeat the tag, " We must import to export ", never pause to ask why or what is the purpose of importing if it is only to export. It is a convenient fallacy, which generally serves to justify the existence of a man's trade, profession, or investments. If this were true, we should have exports, including shipping revenue and imports about balancing. But there is a balance in favour of imports of several hundred millions. Sometimes this is an absolute deficit as well as an apparent deficit amounting to over a hundred millions in a year as in 1931. This absolute deficit is growing once more. We are living on capital. The reason that it does not correspond with the apparent deficit is simply because the most of the apparent deficit in external trading is made up of imports which act as interest in kind on overseas investment. To take only two instances, we have about £200,000,000 invested in China; about £440,000,000 invested in the Argentine. The dividends from such overseas investments are politely called invisible exports. They are, in fact, largely the visible excess of import over export, and as such they serve to keep our men on the dole and to allow city magnates to spread over many countries their risk of losing capital in one.

A regenerated agriculture would undoubtedly imperil part of these investments; financiers and investors would suffer, many of the latter quite

196

modestly placed people. These have been led by the financiers' system to invest money in all ignorance more or less unpatriotically. The more far-sighted and 'liberal-minded' financiers have been well aware that their security is much more assured, if they can induce many thousands of small investors to put their savings in foreign investments. The small man does this generally on the advice of some city firm, or from reading the financial page of his favourite newspaper. These people are worthy of consideration rather than the financier, who thus goes into the commercial battle sheltering behind the widow and the pensioner. The small investor unwittingly becomes the first line of defence in the attack on unemployment. But the restoration of agriculture would not ruin these people, since the increase in livestock would be gradual. So long as we have the present system of investment they will always have other and more patriotic investments available. Nor will we be faced with an immediate financial crisis for the same reason. There is bound to be some loss and some hardship, but nothing worth while is ever accomplished without sacrifice. The better the purpose the more justifiable the sacrifice. In this case there is little doubt that a sacrifice of the less worthy will have to be made for the more worthy who are the productive breadwinners. In war, and at present in peace time, it is the opposite way round.

But it will not only be agriculture which will

gain, it will be the whole of productive industry. The export trade will not suffer, since the Argentine, for instance, has to send her beef here for lack of market elsewhere. She will not, therefore, refuse to buy from us because we take less of her exports than before, she will merely be able to pay fewer dividends to the City of London. A sound trade is one which exchanges goods and services to the mutual benefit of each country. Most invisible exports do not fill this bill. But even so, trade does not necessarily achieve any special virtue by being international. It is of no special benefit that we should send coal to Denmark in return for bacon, when we could send it to our farmers for the same purpose. It would, indeed, be far more stable and beneficial to exchange coal and bacon among our own people at home. Most of the food we import comes in to pay for invisible exports, that is, dividends from abroad. Our manufacturers make no goods in exchange for these, but they would make them in exchange for the products of home agriculture; and so unemployment in industry would be lessened and the wheels of industry would turn. Nearly every farm needs more implements. We would use more coal in light and power as well as in steam-engines, boilers, and threshing machines if farming was more profitable. The writer knows of one 3000-acre arable farm, even in present conditions, which has trebled its use of coal and fuel power by intensifying its livestock; this farm is still capable of using double its present quantity of coal as well as of doubling its investment in buildings, improvements, and machinery if it were possible to farm intensively. The neglect of agriculture is industry's greatest loss. But it is not only the direct benefit to industry which agriculture could give. The indirect benefit is equally as great. A million and a half[1] unemployed men and women are not only living on dole and poor relief, they are capable only of purchasing the barest necessities of life. In work they themselves double their purchases of the products of their fellow-workers. The extra profits of industry and the lightened taxation for unemployment and poor relief would be far greater than any subsidy or protection granted to make agriculture truly prosperous.

Home Agriculture and the Empire

The free trader's last line of defence is the Empire. From Little Englander he has turned to Pygmy Imperialist. Any project to benefit home industry, and especially agriculture, is countered by an appeal to the harmful effects on inter-imperial trade. The Empire, which he has now succeeded in dissolving politically, is the darling of his heart, if it will serve to keep the

[1] The present unemployment figures are slightly lower owing to boom conditions in armaments, but, even so, there are many unemployed still not registered.

gates of foreign trade ajar. But for anyone looking
to the future the fundamental need is to people
with British stocks the waste places in the temperate zones of the map coloured red. In general,
imperial methods of agriculture do not do this.
The land is cultivated for specialized purposes in
enormous areas with practically no permanent
yeoman stock. As a result the desert sets in. Land
is not inanimate raw material, but the living stuff
of life, and unless it be treated as such it dies and
becomes desert. The very worst service that we
can do the Dominions is to encourage them to
exploit their capital fertility in land in order to
export cheap food to us. We have seen how dust
storms and drought have grown in Canada[1] with
millions of acres ruined simply by cultivating
wheat year after year. We have seen in many parts
how rainfall is diminishing through the cutting of
forests either to clear land for agriculture or to
export timber.

Crop disease and insect pests are intensified
likewise by monoculture of crops, both in time
and space. A two-hundred acre wheat field grown
year after year in wheat brings an accumulation of
soil deficiencies. First, it causes erosion and soil
exhaustion, which no artificial manuring can cure
because the humus is gone. Secondly, the plant
itself by being cultivated over a wide area and a
long time in years not only gets no humus but it

[1] See Sir Evelyn Wrench's article, " Canada's Dust Bowl,"
The Times, August 17th, 1937.

struggles for life with its neighbours which need exactly the same plant essentials. Thus it would be weakened even if humus were available. All the natural diseases existing in the ground attack and find the plant too weak to resist. So the crop fails not only because it is weak and poor in itself but because it is the natural prey to disease.

Another very serious aspect of this method of farming is the paucity of labour it employs. There is no approach to true peasant self-contained farming. Two men can cultivate a square mile of ground with only a gang of casual labour for the harvest. This is done for as long as the land lasts and then new land is sought. Thus the natural heritage of ten thousand years is wasted in two generations. On such soil strip-farming, which is alternate fallow and wheat, is nearly as bad from the erosion point of view, unless a green crop is grown between the fallow and wheat to cover the soil. Family farming, which involved selling off just enough crops to buy clothes and other necessities, would have developed and enriched this heritage. But in general nearly all the Dominions can only point to vast spaces underpopulated and over-exploited; although they have here and there startling examples of land preserved in surrounding desert by good farming. Yet they are faced along the whole Pacific with the menace of teeming yellow and brown races. These races are land hungry. We have taught them modern western ways, and in India's case have enabled the population nearly to double itself. We cannot hold them back for ever now that they are awake to western possibilities. They have kept the Oriental fatalism and patience. Loss of life means nothing to them so long as with western weapons they can turn the tables on their western masters at the auspicious moment, which might be the next European war. The only dykes that can hold this flood of humanity are human, yet Canada has little more than the population of greater London to people her vast area of land. Australia has only about half of Canada's population, and New Zealand less than half of Australia's. It may be thought that with Canada's drought-stricken Provinces there is no room for increasing farm population. There would be room, before long, if real farming took place on the unspoiled areas and a systematic effort was made to regenerate the lost lands.

We must cease to waste land by exploitation of its capital and we must people our waste spaces. "We" means the white northern races of Europe united in solidarity to save the new world and Africa by human fertility. Except for South Africa, British stock almost predominates in the Dominions. It is therefore right on biological grounds that we should people the Dominions. For ten years at least we will need most of our pioneer stock for the homeland until our own soil is re-peopled. In the nation building of the new lands there will be better results if we limit our cross-breeding to kindred Nordic stocks from

Scandinavia, Germany, and Holland. These stocks, with our own, are the remnants, somewhat mixed, alas! of the Nordic race which was the begetter of western civilization and achievement even in the halcyon days of Greece. The modern mixed Mediterranean stocks have their own problems on that sea in Abyssinia, North Africa, and South America. Our northern stock has been continually weakened—first in battle for two thousand years, and later by trade, which gave the worst stocks, the people of the ghettos and the bazaar and the Mediterranean types, their opportunity to flourish at the expense of the northern races. We in Britain have spilled our precious, finer blood in three centuries across the world. The only hope to recoup that loss is to give our blood the chance of breeding on the land again at home and in the temperate parts of the Empire. By the sea, and even more by the soil, we have flourished; in the cities we are near to perishing.

Therefore, on the land of England first of all and on the land of the Dominions next, we must replenish our blood. The whole purpose in dealing with the Dominions, for their sake and our's alike, must be to conserve the land and to reproduce fine stocks upon it. This double purpose works hand in hand. The land cannot be made fertile without men upon it, and without land the northern stock dwindles and the cross-breds flourish in the towns.

The question of exporting foodstuffs from the Dominions to ourselves should be a very different one if these two conditions of sound statesmanship are followed. The first is the increase of British and Nordic population in the Dominions, and the second is the spread of that population on the land in homesteads which should be of the self-supporting mixed-farming type. Even if the Dominion populations remain stationary, the only way to save their land from becoming desert will be by mixed farming, which entails far smaller specialized export of cereal and other things than that on which they rely at present.

All things happen gradually on the land. If the Dominions turn soon to yeoman and peasant farming, so will the situation at home alter year by year as we become more self-supporting. A large market will not be cut off suddenly. If at the same time we turn more to our Dominions and less to foreign sources of supply, so will the drop in Dominion exports of agriculture be more gradual. As Denmark and the Argentine lose their markets here, so should the Dominions, after ourselves, take what remains. Thus by the increase in their home population and the decline in competition of foreign exports the Dominions will still be able to exchange most of their surplus foodstuffs for our manufactures: but as time goes on this must be an exchange and not a tribute in kind for old development credits and war loans. It would be not only right but good policy to wipe the Dominions' war debts off the slate. It is these debts and development loans which cause Dominion countries to subsidize exchange depreciation and to produce bad farming.

It may be arrogant on the writer's part to prescribe what methods of farming the Dominions should adopt, but it is an arrogance for which there is no apology. The desert will spread and stay like the Sahara if it is not done. If they do not return to the land wherever space and opportunity offer, the Nordic races will perish and, except in Europe, Asia will take our heritage.

EPITOME

THIS book has tried to show the choice between life and death. It is in our own hearts that we should choose.

There is no safety in war if we cannot feed our people or assure food supplies. There is no safety from war if we cannot fill our bellies and, therefore, we have no independence. None respects the fearful or the fool. As we are now, we are not fearful but fools. We are fools not to be fearful, since nothing will avail us until our rations are in the granary or growing in a soil made bountiful by our service and our foresight. A generation of peace and carelessness has left us only the security of folly. Hence, we must turn to fear. Fear may arouse us before it is too late. It is out of strife that a nation's unity and purpose are made. Unity does not come from the civil war, the loose paunches and the sentimental sadisms of this post-war peace—sadisms which sacrifice the healthy and the strong. But strife brings unity from fear, fear for the future or the intolerable present. It may be our misfortune that in the midst of false prosperity the present has never been intolerable enough, since complacency has not allowed the slow process of decay to fill our hearts with dread, but if we can face the future with fear, we can prepare. Then we will have unity to restore our purpose. Except for that only cataclysm can unite us, and then too late. Yet there is too much sound stock left to have to own we are too late. It is blood and soil which rule at last; but if they fail only anarchy and slavery succeed. Fear is not ignoble if we can restore our heritage more nobly when fear has first united us in purpose. Right purpose will produce right policy. Once more the sound stocks will be protected if necessary by sacrificing the bad stocks. But there is one final necessity for blood which is soil, because without good soil health is impossible. To hope for good stocks to flourish on starving soil is like sowing upon stony ground where the seed springeth up and is cut down. The heights to which our people may attain cannot be won without the health which comes from the soil. Fear for our bellies can bring back health to our bodies if we cultivate our own land. If we neglect it our people will fail even in peace, for food from the wasted lands will not avail. If we serve our soil we can bring back the fertility of the strong breeds that will people the Empire with desired men and women who could hold it against the tides of yellow men and brown.

Britain is an over-populated microcosm of the West. Upon us in the last resort the West depends. Nature has taught us that the land demands balance of crop and livestock and forest, that care and love and human sweat are the wardens of health and soil fertility, that weeds must be watched and destroyed, that disease only thrives when the soil's health loses. If we can regard the human stock of England as we should regard her soil, there are no summits which she may not reach.

THE PRINCIPAL SOURCES AND TONNAGE OF CERTAIN KEY IMPORTS

THE Table of Imports which is printed below is taken from the "Tabular Statement of the Admiralty to accompany B.R.84 (Map showing World Trade)," and this Statement is for *certain* important commodities and was made out in the year 1934. It must be remembered that since that date imports have risen considerably.

In the food group, cocoa, coffee, tea, and sugar might be ignored as not being absolutely necessary for our survival; but these could only be ignored if there were ample supplies of staple foodstuffs available, and they could only be ignored at the expense of great disaffection and discontent among the people, since the use especially of sugar and tea has become a deeply engrained habit which would be hard to break suddenly.

It should be noticed in reading the figures that as things stand at present there is practically not one of the imports quoted which would not be necessary for food or clothing, the munitions industry, or the vital material of essential industries.

One of the most striking things is the immense distances over which many of these necessities have to be carried, and where they are available from neighbouring countries it must be clear how uncertain the supply would be.

The less important sources of supply have not been quoted, though many of them are equally distant or equally difficult of access in time of war. Even if alternative sources of supplies could be rapidly expanded, which is most doubtful, there would be very little difference in the difficulties besetting their transport.

TABLE I

Principal sources of import of various commodities. The total amount imported, in 1000's of tons, is shown in brackets against each commodity.

	1000's of tons		1000's of tons
BARLEY (774)		COCOA (76)	
Iran	165	British West Africa	69
Argentina	135	British West Indies	2
U.S.A. (including Hawaii)	120	COFFEE (27)	
Canada	68	Costa Rica	12
Russia (U.S.S.R.)	39	British East Africa	7
Chile	38	India	2
Australia	29		
		COPPER (279)	
BUTTER (485)		Chile	89
New Zealand	134	Canada	80
Denmark	124	Rhodesia	53
Australia	105	U.S.A. (including Hawaii)	40
Irish Free State	23		
CHEESE (149)			
New Zealand	105	COPPER ORE (41)	
Canada	26	Canada	28

APPENDIX I

COTTON (593)	1000's of tons	JUTE (244)	1000's of tons
U.S.A.	227	India	244
Egypt	123		
India	73	LEAD (316)	
Brazil	64	Australia	164
Peru	39	Canada	77
		India	42
FERTILIZERS (527)		Mexico	16
French Africa	374		
Belgium	38		
Netherlands	31	MAIZE (3205)	
U.S.A. (including		Argentina	2710
Hawaii)	19	British S. and S.W.	
		Africa	148
FLAX (64)		Rumania	101
Russia (U.S.S.R.)	32	Russia (U.S.S.R.)	69
Belgium	20		
		MANGANESE ORE	
HEMP (92)		(202)	
Philippine Islands	42	India	156
British S. and S.W.		British West Africa	26
Africa	27		
Italy	9	MEAT (1533)	
India	5	Argentina	480
		New Zealand	260
IRON ORE (4359)		Denmark	220
French Africa	1436	Australia	193
Spain	1182	Canada	64
Sweden	599	U.S.A. (including	
Norway	410	Hawaii)	57
Spanish Africa	223	Uruguay	47
British West Africa	156	Irish Free State	37
Netherlands	45		
Newfoundland			
(including Coast of		NICKEL (5)	
Labrador)	23	Canada	2

213

OATS (185)	1000's of tons	RICE (128)	1000's of tons
Canada	117	India	65
Russia (U.S.S.R.)	24	French Indo-China	15
Argentina	23	Siam	15
Chile	11		

OIL NUTS, OIL SEEDS, OILS AND FATS (1839)		RUBBER (214)	
Egypt	370	Malaya (Straits Settlements and Malay States)	144
India	268	Netherlands Islands in Indian Ocean	39
Nigeria (including British Cameroons)	215	Ceylon	19
Japan	187		
U.S.A. (including Hawaii)	145	SILK (3)	
		Japan	1
		China	1

PAPER (1044)		
Netherlands	216	SUGAR (2305)
Newfoundland	177	West and East Indies by far the largest source of supply

PETROLEUM AND PETROLEUM PRODUCTS (10,046)		TEA (228)	
Netherlands, West Indies and Guiana	3222	India	124
Iran	2275	Ceylon	70
U.S.A. (including Hawaii)	1257	TIN (10)	
Mexico	1095	Malaya	5
Rumania	716	Dutch East Indies	4
Peru	386		
British West Indies	377	TIN ORE (39)	
Russia (U.S.S.R.)	237	Bolivia	25
Netherlands East Indies	198	Nigeria	8

APPENDIX I

WHEAT (5131)	1000's of tons	WOOL (369)	1000's of tons
Canada	1785	Australia	115
Argentina	1754	New Zealand	97
Australia	1083	British S. and S. W.	
Russia (U.S.S.R.)	105	Africa	48
		Argentina	38
		India	17

WOOD AND TIMBER (8890)		ZINC (149)	
Finland	1977	Canada	77
Russia (U.S.S.R.)	1749	Belgium	30
Sweden	1229	Rhodesia	14
Canada	1158	Australia	10

WOOD PULP AND
ESPARTO (2429)
    Mainly from Sweden,
      Finland, Norway, and
      French Africa

ZINC ORE (90)
    Australia   51
    Newfoundland
      (including Coast of
      Labrador)   32

MISCELLANEOUS STATISTICS

THE tables which follow show the decline in arable acreage over seventy years and the variations in the numbers of livestock kept on the land. In reading these figures the tendencies become plainer if we remember that a given number of younger cattle will not return so much to the soil in dung as the same number of older and bigger animals. Although the dung of dairy cows heavily fed on concentrates may have a high manurial value, the waste of good urine from our modern cowsheds is very great unless that rare amenity, a liquid-manure tank, is installed and used. Moreover, it is at least questionable whether a large number of present-day dairy farmers make the best use of the dung from their cows.

The comparative figures in the returns of older animals applies also to sheep. The consequent loss to the land of fertility is greater even than the statistics show, for the former practice of folding sheep on arable land enriched the soil, but even among the existing smaller numbers of arable sheep the almost universal tendency to kill lambs before their first winter means a relative decrease in the relative number of sheep at the time that they can do most good to the soil. A reference to page 34 of the Ministry of Agriculture and Fisheries Agricultural statistics for 1935 shows most clearly the immense loss in the numbers of arable sheep on the land, which a mere reference to the general figures do not reveal.

Thus when we take into account that there is a loss of well over a million horses in seventy years, and take into account the loss of arable sheep and the extra weight of older animals carried on the soil, there is little difference between the proportion of livestock carried now and seventy years ago. The decline in private horses kept for transport owing to their replacement by the trader and the professional man with the motor-car makes the total figure of the decline probably far higher than a million. Moreover, when nearly every cottager kept a pig, the numbers of these must have run into hundreds of thousands, although they were not recorded in the official returns. But the striking thing in our decline declares itself in the far greater production of cereals in the past without the aid of mineral fertilizers and with insignificant imports of animal feeding-stuffs. This in a large measure is a proof that by return to sound methods of husbandry and more intensive cultivation by increased labour on the land, we can make better use of our organic manure and so produce a far larger quantity of food for the population at the same time as we reduce our imports of animal foodstuffs.

TABLE II

ARABLE ACREAGE

INCLUDING GRASS IN ROTATION

	GREAT BRITAIN	ENGLAND AND WALES
1867	17,695,475	14,369,212
1936	12,095,761	9,119,766
DECREASE	5,599,714	5,249,446

The acreages in 1867 and in 1936 of the two main root crops fed to animals are shown in Table III :

TABLE III

	TURNIPS AND SWEDES	MANGOLDS
1867		
Great Britain	2,173,850	258,126
England and Wales	1,688,050	257,282
1936		
Great Britain	795,147	249,219
England and Wales	449,276	246,017

Thus there was a total decrease in the two crops in Great Britain of 1,387,610 acres, and in England and Wales of 1,250,039 acres.

On the other hand, certain green crops have

218

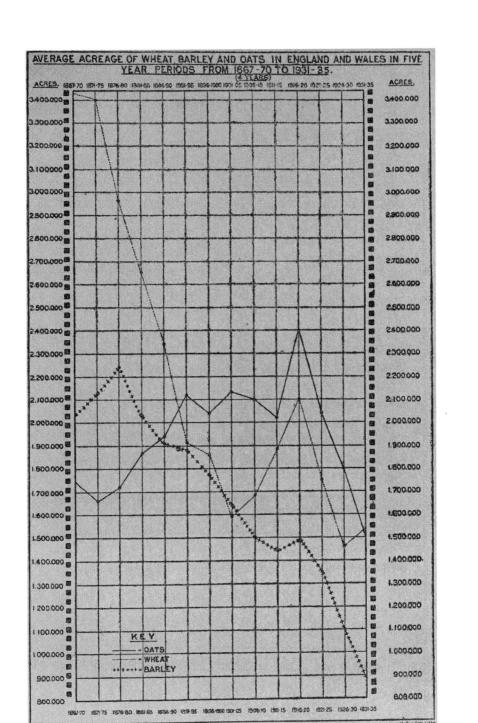

AVERAGE ACREAGE OF WHEAT, BARLEY AND OATS IN ENGLAND AND WALES IN FIVE YEAR PERIODS FROM 1867-70 TO 1931-35.
(4 YEARS)

KEY
——— OATS
– – – WHEAT
+ + + + + BARLEY

WHEAT: 3,256,758 acres 1867; 1,704,469 acres 1936; decrease 1,552,289 acres.
BARLEY: 2,040,678 acres 1867; 818,943 acres 1936; decrease 1,221,735 acres.
OATS: 1,753,367 acres 1867; 1,419,870 acres 1936; decrease 333,497 acres.

increased, the acreage under cabbages, kohl-rabi, and rape being given in Great Britain in 1867 as 133,692, and in England and Wales as 129,542, whereas in 1936 there were 175,625 acres under this heading in England and Wales, and Great Britain had 63,140 acres of rape alone.

But the increase in cabbages, kohl-rabi and rape (in England and Wales 46,983 acres) does not compensate for the decline in the fodder root crops, and in addition there has been a marked increase in green and beet crops (all of which are 'greedy' feeders and take a great deal, especially in humus, out of the land) sold for cash off the farm, directly or indirectly for human consumption.

In 1914 there were only 2334 acres of sugar-beet in England and Wales, but by 1936 this had increased to 348,659 acres. (It is admitted that 211,622 tons of plain dried pulp were produced for fodder, as a by-product from the manufacture of sugar.)

In 1922 the acreage in England and Wales and under carrots, onions, cabbage for human consumption, brussels sprouts, cauliflower or broccoli, rhubarb and celery was 82,021; in 1936 the acreage was 131,662, an increase of 49,641 acres.

ROUGH GRAZINGS

The first year in which an official estimate was made of the extent of rough grazings was 1892, when the acreage for Great Britain was given as 12,087,232 acres. By 1898 the figure was 12,856,938 acres, but some of the increase may have been due to greater accuracy in the returns under this heading.

In 1931 the rough grazing acreage in Scotland was 9,497,263 acres. In 1932 it was given as 10,368,178 acres, an increase of 870,915 acres. This increase was mainly accounted for by the fact that on this occasion land in deer forests used, or capable of being used, for grazing, estimated at 1,028,666 acres was included, whereas in previous years only the acreage in deer forests returned as *used for grazing* was included under this head.

Table IV gives an indication of the increase of rough grazings since 1898 in Great Britain.

TABLE IV

YEAR	ACRES
1898	12,856,938
1914	12,929,124
1921	13,937,302
1927	15,022,805
1936	15,844,169

TABLE V

NUMBER OF VARIOUS KINDS OF LIVESTOCK IN GREAT BRITAIN IN THE YEARS 1867 AND 1936.

| | SHEEP | | | PIGS |
	1 YEAR OLD AND OVER	UNDER ONE YEAR	TOTAL	
1867	18,449,005	10,470,096	28,919,101	2,966,979
1936	13,190,782[1]	11,014,641	24,205,423	4,040,176

[1] This includes 10,548,232 ewes kept for breeding. In 1867 there was no such differentiation made in the returns for sheep over 1 year old.

AGE OF LIVESTOCK

The practice of selling animals for slaughter at an earlier age than formerly has grown over a considerable period, and this is true of cattle, sheep, and pigs.

Thus the increase in the total number of cattle has taken place in cows and heifers and in " Other Cattle " under two years, while " Other Cattle " of two years and over have decreased.

Table VI taken from *Agricultural Statistics* of 1934 shows how these tendencies have developed in England and Wales.

TABLE VI

Table showing the average ages of Cattle taken from the Agricultural Statistics of 1934.

Period	Average Dairy Herd	Average number of other cattle			Average Total Cattle
		Two years and over	Under two years	Total other cattle	
1867–71	1,733,000	1,088,000	1,441,000	2,529,000	4,262,000
1910–14	2,365,000	1,091,000	2,387,000	3,478,000	5,843,000
1930–34	2,858,000	977,000	2,476,000	3,453,000	6,311,000

BRITISH OVERSEAS INVESTMENTS

(Extract from Parliamentary Debates,
May 3, 1937)

MAJOR DORMAN-SMITH asked the President of the Board of Trade the total amount of British capital now invested in countries overseas, and the amount of such capital invested in Canada, including Newfoundland, Australia and New Zealand, the Union of South Africa, and Argentina.

DR. BURGIN replied: " No official estimates of British investments overseas are available. But according to a tentative estimate based on careful but not yet fully completed research, which I have obtained through the courtesy of Sir Robert Kindersley, the total amount of British oversea investments is about £3,800,000,000. The amount of British-owned securities and private investments in Canada, including Newfoundland, being £520,000,000, Australia £540,000,000, New Zealand £140,000,000, the Union of South Africa £280,000,000, and the Argentine £440,000,000."

SUBSIDIES AND AGRICULTURAL INDEBTEDNESS

THE student of agricultural matters will be familiar, in some degree at least, with the fact that many, if not all, the countries which export staple foodstuffs to Great Britain have in various ways during the past few years from time to time subsidized their exports.

But the charge has so often been levied against British farmers that they cannot compete on equal terms with foreign or Dominion farmers that it may not be out of place here to give a few examples of foreign and Dominion subsidies.

What follows is not intended to be exhaustive or even necessarily up to date. It must be remembered that subsidies may take many and varied forms. It would require the work of a squad of statisticians to summarize the assistance given to world agriculture in exports for a single year. There are, for example, shipping subsidies which may operate indirectly to subsidize exports, and there are the currency manipulations of which examples have already been touched on in Chapter IX.

For details of the more direct forms of subsidy

the reader is particularly referred to publications of the International Institute of Agriculture and of the Imperial Economic Committee. In examining the following examples it is important to note how often the regulated home price is considerably in excess of the subsidized export price. Some of these examples are not large in themselves, but we must not forget that one cheap shipment can influence the whole general market in Great Britain until it is disposed of.

NOTE.—The sources of information are denoted by their initials:

G.M. *Government Measures affecting Agricultural Prices, an International Quarterly Summary of Government Measures affecting the prices of Cereals, Meats and Dairy Products,* published by the International Institute of Agriculture.

D.P.S. *Dairy Produce Supplies,* 1936.

A.E.S. *Agricultural Economics and Sociology.*

[Italics throughout this Appendix are mine.]

AUSTRALIA
See G.M. (1935), No. 3.

" Position on December 31st, 1934.

" The Government has made arrangements for the provision of financial assistance to wheat growers and for the *payment of a bounty on the production of wheat.* Under the Wheat Growers' Relief (No. 2) Act, 1934, assistance is paid to any wheat grower at the rate of 3s. for each acre sown by him for wheat during the year 1934.

"Under the Wheat Bounty Act, 1934, a bounty at the rate of 3*d*. per bushel is paid on wheat which has been harvested between October 1st, 1934, and March 31st, 1935, and sold between October 1st, 1934, and October 31st, 1935. . . .

"A total of £870,000 was paid *in relief* to wheat growers during the nine months ending March 31, 1935."

There was also a discrimination in taxation.

"Under the Flour Tax Acts, 1934, a tax of £2 12*s*. 6*d*. per short ton is imposed on flour manufactured and sold, delivered or used by any person; on flour in excess of 1000 lbs. held in stock by any person; on flour, biscuits, cakes, macaroni, etc., imported into Australia on and after January 7th, 1935, and before January 7th, 1936. Provision is made that no commodity is taxed twice. The flour tax imposed on home-grown flour is not payable *when the flour is sold for export* or used for consumption in the Northern Territory, or when it is used in the preparation of certain wheat products."

CANADA
See G.M. (1936), No. 8.

"The Canadian Wheat Board was set up in 1935 by an Act of Parliament, with the following powers: (*a*) to buy wheat from producers at *fixed minimum prices*; (*b*) to sell wheat in the export markets as advantageously as possible; (*c*) to assume ownership of all stocks of domestic wheat in Canada; (*d*) to control grain elevators and to regulate their relations with transport agencies. While the Grain Board Act is applicable to grains other than wheat, no steps have as yet been taken to establish control over the marketing of such grains.

" Producers are not compelled to sell to the Board at the guaranteed minimum price. If the Board finds it possible over the entire season to sell the wheat at a price averaging more than the fixed price, producers are entitled to a *pro rata* share in such a surplus. No special provision is made for covering any losses resulting from the sale of wheat at a price averaging less than the fixed price. [*The assumption is that such losses would be a direct charge on the Treasury.*] The Board is empowered to utilize all existing marketing channels in its operations, and in addition, may establish its own marketing facilities."

IRISH FREE STATE
See G.M. (1935), No. 2.

The " Slaughter of Cattle and Sheep Act " of September 13th, 1934, was brought into operation in October of that year in order to remedy the situation brought about by the imposition of quotas by the British Government on Irish cattle.

It was estimated that the annual cost of carrying

the Act into effect would be £600,000, of which £400,000 would be used for the provision of free beef. At the same time a levy was imposed on cattle and sheep killed for human consumption in the Irish Free State; the levies were expected to realize £300,000 per annum.

Bounties were paid on exports of meat in 1934 as follows:

Cattle	£599,868
Live pigs	£68,489
Fresh pork	£93,473
Bacon	£396,380

"The Dairy Produce (Price Stabilization) Acts of 1932 and 1933 provide for the imposition of levies on butter produced in the Irish Free State and for the payment of export bounties on butter and other milk products. . . ." During 1934 there were paid out in export bounties under the Acts £1,164,106 on butter and £26,193 on other milk products. In addition, other export bounties and subsidies were paid out of monies provided by the Government as follows: £785,829 on butter and £38,574 on other milk products.

NEW ZEALAND

The following is a *précis* of information from D.P.S., 1936, p. 63:

Under the Primary Products Marketing Act,

1936, the Minister of Marketing was empowered to acquire all dairy produce intended for export at prices fixed on the basis of the average of eight to ten preceding years. The Minister was also empowered to acquire dairy produce for consumption in New Zealand and to fix internal prices.

ARGENTINA

MEAT AND GENERAL MEASURES
See G.M. 1937, No. 9.

" The Argentine Government have issued a decree subsidizing Beef exports to the United Kingdom. For every pound sterling derived from the shipments of various kinds of beef arriving in Great Britain after December 16th, 1936, 1.65 pesos will be credited to the National Meat Board from the Exchange Profits Fund, to a maximum of 15,100,000 pesos a year.[1]

" The subsidy will be distributed among exporting firms in proportion to shipments to the United Kingdom, and measures are being taken to ensure that the stock-breeders also receive the benefit of the subsidy.

" The preamble describes the measure as a tem-

---

[1] " In this way the exporter, who otherwise would be obliged to sell his export bills as a fixed rate of 15 pesos to the £, will receive instead 16.65 pesos. Generally the Government sells this foreign exchange to importers at a rate of 16 pesos to the £; therefore under this plan it loses 0.65 peso per £. As the subsidy is limited to

porary expedient, and observes that a subsidy is justifiable only in the case of a passing crisis or for the maintenance of an industry contending against adverse natural conditions. In the present case, State intervention should be limited to avoiding dislocation due to a sudden change in the United Kingdom import system."

Dairy Industry (D.P.S. 1936)

Under a governmental decree the National Board of Control for the Dairy Industry was set

---

15,100,000 pesos, about 73 per cent. of these meat exports will get the profit arising from it.

"While Argentina has never applied quotas to imports, she exercises a close control over the foreign exchange market which in practice works in a similar way. It should be observed, however, that this control does not hinder the repatriation of foreign funds from Argentina, and since 1934 there have been practically no blocked funds in the country.

"There are two foreign exchange markets in Argentina: (1) The official market, with different buying and selling rates, the latter applying in the case of imports for which *foreign exchange permits are granted*. The difference between the two rates, about 6.66 per cent., accrues to a special fund for facilitating the Argentine grain exports and covering exchange losses on the service of external debt. (2) The free market, on which the peso rate is slightly lower than on the official market.

"All exchange operations which cannot be carried out on the official market can be effected on the free market without restriction. However, imports without special exchange permits pay a rate 20 per cent. higher than the official sellers' rate."

up in April 1934. Its functions were to secure for the primary producers the full value of export bills for butter and casein.

The receipts of the Board for 1935 totalled 5,267,000 pesos, made up of 3,153,000 pesos from the margin on foreign exchange and 2,114,000 pesos from the levy on locally consumed butter. During the year 4,914,000 pesos were paid to producers as premiums on their sales of butter fat.

DENMARK
(D.P.S. 1936)

No direct aid was granted to the Danish dairy industry until near the end of 1933, although the varying prices obtained for butter on different export markets were equalized by means of a pooling arrangement.

In May 1937 a temporary plan for the relief of the industry was put into operation. This takes the form of a guaranteed minimum price to farmers for butter for home consumption, rising from 220 Kr. to 250 Kr. per 100 kg. and is financed by a Butter Fund, the revenues of which are derived partly from a levy on home sales (the difference between the home price and the export price), and *partly from a direct Government subsidy of 25 Kr. per 100 kg.*, provision being made for a reduction in payments when the Copenhagen quotation rises above the fixed figure.

In addition, *a sum up to 3,000,000 Kr. may be received om the Treasury* to provide milk for needy persons at the reduced rate during the validity of the Act, while up to 3,000,000 Kr. may be lent to the dairy organizations for the erection of cold stores, chiefly for butter. The Act is intended to operate during the current year only, after which it is hoped to introduce a long-term plan for agriculture as a whole.

In view of a material restriction of Denmark's export markets for cattle and beef and the low prices of dairy products, a scheme has been in force since 1932 for the destruction of cattle at fixed prices, financed by a levy on killings for domestic consumption; a considerable proportion of the number so slaughtered has consisted of old and diseased dairy cows. Approximately 130,000 animals were slaughtered under the scheme in 1933, 150,000 in 1934, 74,000 in 1935, and 96,000 in 1936.

ESTONIA
(D.P.S. 1936)

Measures to offset the low prices to which Estonian butter had fallen were contained in a law passed in January 1934. Under this law the price of butter was fixed at 1.50 Kr. per kg., and in order to maintain this price a fund was created, financed by monies transferred from various special funds and from general State revenues. The home price is maintained at a figure varying from *25 cents to 30 cents per kg. above the export price.*

In order to secure and maintain foreign markets the Minister of Agriculture was empowered to fix the amounts which exporters must sell on each separate market. The Government can withhold export bounties from butter exporters who do not comply with these conditions. The total amount paid in export bounties during the year 1934 was approximately 3,200,000 Kr.; during the fiscal year ended April 1936, bounties paid amounted to only 550,000 Kr., and in the succeeding year payments were probably only about half this amount.

The law regulating the payment of export bounties on dairy produce, which previously had provided for bounties on butter and cheese only, was amended at the end of 1936 in order to include bounties on exports of condensed milk and milk powder.

FINLAND
(D.P.S. 1936)

The amounts expended on bounties for butter and cheese have been as follows:

BUTTER			CHEESE		
		marks			marks
1933	...	35,552,000	1933	...	5,729,000
1934	...	66,966,000	1934	...	6,899,000
1935	...	49,700,000	1935	...	10,360,000
1936	...	66,300,000	1936	...	10,580,000

Meat. See G.M. (1936), No. 5.

Bounties were also paid on the export of live pigs, cattle, and pigs meat.

LATVIA
(D.P.S. 1936)

By a decree issued in August 1930, a sum of money was set aside for the payment of bounties to butter producers. Under this plan the Ministry of Agriculture were to award bounties to producers for milk delivered to dairies making butter for export.

The sums disbursed by the State in giving assistance to producers of export butter averaged about 20,000,000 Ls. annually from 1932 to 1935, but were under 6,000,000 Ls. in 1936.

NETHERLANDS
(D.P.S. 1936)

The Netherlands is a large net exporter of butter, but imports began to increase in 1931, and control of importation by quota has been in operation since April 1932.

The amount paid out in the form of assistance to producers of dairy produce totalled 91,041,000 florins in 1936 as against 97,270,000 florins in the preceding year; refund of levies on butter exported amounted to 47,791,000 florins as compared with 41,586,000 florins in 1935.

A plan to limit the number of cows, and so aid

the market for milk as well as for beef, has been in operation since October 1933, the intention being to reduce the cow population by 200,000. During the period October 1933, to March 1934, over 119,000 cattle were slaughtered, the meat produced being tinned and distributed to the poor. The scheme was then suspended on the ground of the expense involved, but in the autumn of 1934 the Government decided to slaughter another 150,000 head of cattle. Slaughtering was continued until April 1935, when the desired reduction of the cattle population was achieved. The controlling authority, the Cattle Central, also decided that in order to restrict production, the number of calves born in 1936 to be retained in the herds would be limited to 350,477; for 1937 the number has been fixed at 353,300.

Other measures to help the dairying industry included an attempt to increase the consumption of liquid milk by means of propaganda directed to that end and the distribution of cheap margarine to the unemployed; no butter is contained in the margarine thus disposed of. In addition, after March 31st, 1935, it was made compulsory for factories to return to producers in the form of skimmed milk a certain percentage of milk delivered to them. The Dairy Produce Central was empowered to determine this percentage and fix a maximum price for the skimmed milk which, it was hoped, would be utilized as a cheap feeding-stuff.

In certain areas in the West prices of milk for liquid consumption, when sold under Government contract, are fixed by the Government. Three quality grades are recognized.

In spite of attempts to limit production the volume of milk available has increased, as poor-yielding animals have been slaughtered and farmers have tended to retain older cows. The production of butter has risen steadily, amounting to 2,069,000 cwts. (including butter in the margarine *mélange*) in 1936, against 2,036,000 cwts. in 1935.

Meat. See G.M. (1935), No. 1.

"Position on December 31st, 1934.

". . . The importation of live cattle from abroad had already been forbidden before the crisis. The exportation now is assisted, as a means of reducing the number of cattle, by an export bounty which averages 70 fl. per head. . . ."

POLAND

As an example of an ingenious method of indirect subsidy the following may be cited from G.M. (1936), No. 6:

CEREAL EXPORTS

" *Cereal exports are facilitated by a remission of import duties on fertilizers used in cereal production.*

The latest changes in these premiums are given in the following table Zlotys per quintal:

	Before 1/8/36	As from 1/8/36
Wheat, rye, barley oats	6.00	5.00
Flour: ash content 0.0–0.8% ...	10.00	9.00
Flour: ash content 0.8–2.5% ...	8.00	7.00
Flour: ash content 2.5–3.5% ...	5.50	4.00
Barley groats	12.00	9.00
Oat flakes and groats	9.00	8.00
Malt	3.00	3.00

The saving resulting from the lower rates of premium are to be employed in aiding other branches of agriculture."

SWEDEN
(D.P.S. 1936)

During each of the past three years the average export price for Swedish butter and the price fixed for the home market have been as follows:

(Kr. per 100 kg.)

	Export price	Home price
1934 ...	116	230
1935 ...	154	223
1936 ...	175	221

A Royal decree of June 30th, 1932, which came into force on September 20th, 1932, contained provisions for improving the organization of the sale of milk and dairy produce by the imposition of levies.

The sums derived from the levies on milk and other dairy produce and paid into the Price Equalization Fund amounted to over 50,000,000 Kr. in 1935. The amount paid out in subsidizing the export of butter totalled 15,000,000 Kr., while 40,000 Kr. was expended on exports of other dairy produce.

A special fund, the Agricultural Price Regulation Fund, was created in 1935. Into it are paid the proceeds of the various duties imposed for the purpose of regulating prices, such as import and export duties and excise taxes on feeding-stuffs, margarine, etc. The proceeds of each of these taxes are to be used to support that branch of industry in whose interest it is imposed, e.g. the proceeds of import duties on feeding-stuffs are used to support the production of meat and eggs. During the period July 1st, to December 31st, 1935, the revenues of the fund amounted to 14,829,000 Kr. and the disbursements to 18,000,000 Kr. It is estimated that during the fiscal year ended June 30th, 1936, the total revenue of the fund was 26,000,000 Kr. as compared with 20,000,000 Kr. in the preceding year.

SWITZERLAND
See G.M., No. 7

" As the production of milk is of great economic importance the Government has endeavoured, over a long period of years, to *guarantee a reason-*

able selling price to producers. A considerable sum is placed at the disposal of the Federal Council each year. A Federal decree of May 25th, 1936, provides for the following revenue during the period May 1st, 1936, to April 30th, 1937.

(a) *A sum of Fr.* 10,000,000 *provided out of current revenue.*

(b) The net profit of ' Butyra ' including the yield of the Supplementary Import Duties and surcharges levied on butter from May 1st, 1936, to April 30th, 1937, according to the instructions of the Council.

(c) The yield of the levy on liquid milk *(Centime de crise)* produced by non-organized producers from May 1st, 1936, to April 30th, 1937.

(d) The yield of the Supplementary duties and surcharges levied on feeding-stuffs from May 1st, 1936, to April 30th, 1937.

" The sums available from (a), (b), and (c), and two-thirds of (d), are allocated to the Central Milk Producers' Union under conditions to be fixed by the Federal Council to meet the expense of maintaining milk prices during the period from May 1st, 1936, to April 30th, 1937. The remainder (one-third of (d)) is allocated to enable the Federal Council to take other measures for

alleviating the agricultural crisis, and especially
for facilitating the sale of livestock raised in mountain regions.

"*This method or organization has been instru-
mental in maintaining domestic prices of dairy
products considerably higher than export prices.
However, such prices are only paid on certain
quantities of milk so as to limit production.*"

AGRICULTURAL INDEBTEDNESS

Agricultural indebtedness is a matter of urgency
in nearly every country in the world with a developed agriculture. In most cases it has reached
staggering proportions, sometimes as great as the
value of the land itself. The mere fact that the
world's farmers, in nearly every case, are in debt,
means that a large part of that debt has been
formed to tide over losses in agricultural production. This in itself is a proof that the world has
had its food at less than the costs of production,
plus a living wage to the farmer. In general, a
farmer does not borrow money like a limited liability company to float a new venture, he borrows
it because he cannot carry on his existing business
without that help. The more he is in debt the
more he must rob his land to pay interest, and so
the vicious circle of land exploitation proceeds.

If it is impossible to assess the world debts of
farmers it is possible to examine a few of the

methods taken to relieve farmers in other countries, and thus to subsidize indirectly their exports which had previously been subsidized by the provision of credit against past losses.

From the point of view of methods of solution of the problem of agricultural debts States may be roughly grouped into three principal classes.

" The first class includes those States that have taken radical measures aiming directly at relieving the farmers from the burden of their debts. The second is formed by States that have, it is true, pursued a policy of direct intervention in regard to the problem of agricultural debts, but have confined their measures within narrower limits, endeavouring to relieve the debtors without, however, seriously affecting the interests of the creditors. The third class includes those States that have sought to help the debtors mainly by indirect means, or by a general policy of strengthening and protecting agricultural economy, but without violating the principle of respect for obligations incurred.

" The first type of policy and of legislation prevails in certain countries of Central and Eastern Europe. It is characterized by the compulsory conversion of the farmers' debts, a reduction of the rate of interest and sometimes even of the capital sum due being imposed by law.

" The second type of policy and of legislation which in certain countries is distinct from the first, and, in others, is associated with it, takes the form of a series of measures providing for the repayment of the loans by instalments over a series of years, the suspension of measures of distraint against the debtors, the bringing about, through special procedure, of direct arrangements between debtors and creditors, the repayment by the State of part of the debts, the imposition of minimum prices for the sale of expropriated property, and so on.

"Lastly, the third type of policy and legislation is generally adopted by States with a more highly organized economic structure; they endeavour to avoid, as far as possible, any intervention of the public authorities to modify compulsorily the terms and conditions of the legal obligations arising out of the financing of farms, and rather to relieve agriculture from the burden of excessive indebtedness by general action to support and improve agricultural economy.

"It is needless to say that the plans for the adjustment of debts have involved the Governments in financial operations, often on a large scale." [1]

The above quotation implies that in some countries at least, drastic steps were taken by the Governments concerned with a view to lightening the burden of agricultural indebtedness; and when the question of subsidies is under consideration, those steps should be taken into account in assess-

[1] See A.E.S., 1937, No. 1, pp. 11–12.

ing the aid given to agriculture. It is beyond the scope of this appendix, even if it were possible at all, to give anything approaching a complete list of examples of this form of Government relief, but the following, from Europe only, show some of the tendencies.

DENMARK

See A.E.S., 1937, No. 2.

"In 1933, the *total mortgage debt* on rural property was calculated as being 3,750,000,000 crowns, whereas the aggregate value of the farms was 5,400,000,000 crowns . . ."

"In order to lighten the burden of the taxes and mortgage interest payable by owners and tenants of farms, Parliament granted, by a Law dated October 19th, 1931, a sum of 30,000,000 crowns, to be distributed according to determined principles."

"More than 135,000 farmers, that is, 67 per cent. of all the farmers of the country, proved that they were entitled to receive a subsidy under the terms of this Law. The sum of 30,000,000 crowns being insufficient to satisfy the demand, a law voted in 1932 increased the grant, and in all about 42,000,000 crowns were distributed."

A number of other measures were put into operation including postponement of payment, conversion of loans to lower rates of interest, establishment of a fund for granting new loans, and fixing of a maximum rate of interest on loans granted on the security of real property unless a special authorization had been obtained.

HUNGARY
See A.E.S., 1937, No. 3.

By the middle of 1932 agricultural land in Hungary was very heavily burdened with debt. Various steps were taken by the Government, including suspension of sales by auction, contribution by the State towards the payment of interest on debts burdening certain classes of agricultural property, amortization of arrears of taxes, assumption by the State of part of the debts in certain cases, etc.

LATVIA
See A.E.S., 1937, No. 3.

In Latvia, where admittedly the reconstruction of farms destroyed by the war entailed recourse to credit, the amount of the loans completely or partly cancelled amounted, at the end of 1935, to 38,400,000 lats, that is, 15 per cent. of the total of the loans granted.

THE GOVERNMENT
AGRICULTURAL POLICY

THERE are doubtless staunch party men who say that the Government has done, and is doing, all that is necessary for agriculture, who will point to quotas, subsidies and research grants, add the tale of State munificence on their fingers, and then declaim on the farmers' traditional ingratitude. This is justifiable if we take things on their face value and forget the arguments in the previous pages.

The Government itself exposes this fundamental ignorance of the problem by saying that its peace-time proposals are not meant to put agriculture on a war-time basis. By this it can only mean that they do not intend that the land shall be fertile and pro-ductive enough to be able to supply most of our wants when forced by war-time measures. It is the equivalent of saying we will not have an army or a navy fit for war, that the army will be used for tattoos, ceremonial, and charity; the navy will be used for fireworks off Spithead, but as for war it would be too expensive to have defence forces that could defend us. This has been partly true of our attitude towards our forces until the last two years.

Hence, we are faced with the necessity to spend £1,500,000,000 in five years to repair the neglect of fifteen years, but in agriculture, which we have seen to be vital for defence, what we require is that enough shall be done to repair the neglect of fifty years. The cost, however, would be a fraction of the sum needed for armaments, and could itself be highly productive. That this is not contemplated is obvious from the Government's announcements. Properly speaking, agriculture on a war-time basis means that agricultural practice has temporarily to be altered to exploit to the full its peace-time reserves of fertility. In this sense, except that there are no reserves of fertility, agriculture may be considered as already on a war-time basis, since the land is still being exploited, for farmers have to adapt themselves to any doubtful experiment which can keep them out of the bankruptcy court. The great revolutionary changes, generally for the worse in agricultural practice to-day, the much-encouraged and much-praised adaptability of farmers is sufficient proof of instability of policy, markets, and lack of governmental purpose.

It is useless to criticize the Government policy unless one understands such a lack of purpose. In the first place, the Government gets elected through the party machine by bidding for votes. The agricultural vote is scattered as well as small, and the party caucuses, to some extent rightly, consider it can affect very few seats. Each party thinks (while it pursues the basic policy of its opponents) that its existence in power is vital to the country. This is the party man's doctrine of " indispensability ". For him it is never worth the risk of losing office for five years in pursuit of a great purpose, if by being all things to most voters he can keep in power. The very nature of electioneering and vote cadging dulls men's minds to the longer view. Party tactics and big fishing in little waters sooner or later makes politicians quite genuinely blind to the realities and principles which should guide their policies. Any genuine improvement that is essential but difficult is put aside with the comfortable assurance that it is not practical politics. But it is the so-called practical politics of the last thirty years that has led this country into such a false position. No one could doubt the high ideals, the unswerving rectitude, and the good intentions of our present Prime Minister and many of his Cabinet. But as men almost born into modern business and a townsman's attitude to life, it would be nearly impossible for them to connect their ideals to the realities of the soil.

That is the political side of the question. Then it must be remembered that there have been in eight years five different Ministers of Agriculture, few of them with anything but a second-hand knowledge of the soil; all of them professional politicians, two of them doctors. This has meant that they have had to deal with a Cabinet indifferent to agriculture and with a party organization subscribed to largely by traders and City men; above all things the Ministers of Agriculture have been improperly equipped with knowledge of the soil. Thus they have been at the mercy of an admirable Civil Service. But alas, the Ministry of Agriculture naturally has its being in the bureaucratic grooves of socialism. Its members are necessarily more distinguished by their honours in examinations than their practical knowledge of the land. There is no political G.H.Q. thinking out the principles and practice involved. There is no one to present alternatives to the nationalized bureaucracy of the Marketing Board. But there *is* a Board of Trade whose rewards come by the statistics of exports and trade agreements, and there *is* a Treasury which holds as tightly as possible on to the purse strings, when politically unpopular hands would dip into the money-bags. These two departments together with nearly every member of the Cabinet are the enemies of agriculture in fact, if not in intention. Then the worst indirect foe of all is the Ministry of Health. Often this Ministry is devoted to saving the unfit at the expense of the fit, and to spreading urban ideals. Milk regulations, rural housing regulations, and medical officers of health in well-meaning ignorance of anything to do with the country add to the farmers' burdens and his men's difficulties till they are well nigh intolerable.

Thus it is not surprising that most agricultural legislation is a jumble of opposites and desperate last-minute expedients.

These are the reasons why a whole considered

policy for all of agriculture has never taken place, and why the embryo socialism of marketing boards has been the first attention instead of turning to the soil. There is little doubt that the present Minister of Agriculture, if he could have control, would probably go far towards reversing the situation. But he has the gallery of democratic politics, for which he must play. He has actor managers and promoters who do not understand the part for which he is so well cast. He will not be allowed to carry the show on his shoulders. In the first place, he has a multitude of sins to expiate on his predecessors' behalf.

Until Mr. Morrison's advent, except for the protection afforded to fruit and vegetables and hops, nothing whatever fundamental was done. The pig policy took with one hand and gave with the other, and ended in the farmers, who contracted to produce bacon, seeing the curers offering more on the open market for pigs than the farmers received themselves by contract for pigs often produced at a loss. The curers' profits were treated tenderly as were the Dane and other importers of bacon, but the farmer was left with rising food costs and lowered bacon prices. Yet the Government had induced the farmer to co-operate by the implication of protection from quotas, which were not allowed to function. Pig policies will take a lot of untangling, and the farmer is going to be slow to trust himself to promises again. For this he will be branded as grumbling, ungrateful, and short-sighted, as he was

when the last contract failed to secure the right
number of non-existent pigs for a contract which
promised better conditions.

At the time of writing the breeding sows are
being slaughtered rapidly, and the farmers find cold
comfort in the general assurance given that something will be done; they have heard it before.
Although those who know the Minister realize that
he would not have made the promises unless he had
something definite in view, yet it is hard for the
farmer, betrayed steadily since the repeal of the
Corn Production Act, to believe him. It is hard
also for those who realize how much competition
the Minister will have in the Cabinet to believe
that much will be done in the face of trade agreements and rearmament demands. The one will pre-
clude reasonable protection and the other adequate
subsidy.

Until the Milk Board can be disentangled from
its holographs, adding machines and trade-enforced
tyrannies, there will never be any milk policy which
is part of general agriculture. The Milk Board,
when it was formed, had to create a State socialism
as a substitute for organic co-operation. Farmers
bound themselves together to sell milk and to
compel backsliders on the implicit understanding
that, having shown their willingness to co-operate,
they would get protection. Apart from the repeal
of the Corn Production Act there has never been
such a thorough-going cynical betrayal of farmers
and consumers as there has been over the Milk

Board. Far from getting any adequate protection, the Board of Trade won a series of handsome victories for foreign competition. The farmers combined, but, since there was no serious protection from foreign milk products, they have only been able to reduce individual quality of production and play into the hands of the milk distributors. These last have made enormous profits, for their risks have been removed by the Milk Board subsidizing the large distributors, who have turned their marginal milk into milk products. There is a slight temporary improvement and undoubtedly the west of England has gained. The small distributor, who has less than 500 gallons a day of surplus milk for manufacture, has been pushed out of business wherever possible.

The result of the Milk Board has been to set up a bureaucracy at Thames House where one hundred and forty-odd thousand producers have centralized accounts. They fill in forms which would tax a lawyer to understand; and the Board writes many million letters a year. All this by its very nature is a clumsy, inelastic form of nationalization. It is not liked by the farmers, who are the natural producers of liquid milk, and except for an annual producers' meeting, is utterly outside their control. It is not co-operation but bureaucracy.

On farming it has had three main results, all bad. In the first place it has removed the farmer from his customer; quality and freshness from local supplies have, except for producer retailers, failed to count in the same personal way. The personal incentive to good production has disappeared, and it is not compensated for by the penny bonus given for accredited milk. Secondly, it has rendered the producer retailers' position much more insecure; and it is the good producer retailer who is most desirable for milk supplies in small towns and suburbs. He might have been the basis for future co-operation, and he is the man who might have proved the value of clean, fresh milk instead of the bulked half-cooked mixture which is all that most townsmen can get to-day. Thirdly, it has enabled the distant farmers in the north and west countries to turn from cheese-, butter-making, and beef-store breeding, to liquid milk production at the expense of the natural liquid milk producers. It has destroyed the ancient craft of farmhouse cheese-making and butter-making, which again should have been the basis of good co-operation; and, above all, it has made for bad milk ranching by small farmers instead of good farming. Its results are patent in the deterioration of a great part of the western districts. Its results are also apparent in the bad farming of those near towns, who can no longer afford to do their dairy farms as well as before, since they have to pay for the new milk producers elsewhere by a levy to keep up the general pool price for all.

This is not to say that, if there had been no Milk Board, things would have been better for the farmers, who were facing ruin. Fresh milk paid the fortnightly wage bill and cheese and butter production did not, and in consequence the liquid milk market was saturated.[1]

This is not a criticism on members and officials of the Board itself which produced prodigies of organization in a very difficult task. But it is an example of how to do everything wrong by a Government that could not understand the land or care to save it, while more popular alternatives existed and the vested interests could have their way.

The result to the consumer has been that many small and often good distributors can no longer serve them; they must drink bulked cemeteries of cooked germs without any choice or cheapening of the product. The country folk, who could well have had milk fresher and much cheaper, have had to pay urban prices, and have, because the farmer can no longer easily supply them, to get stale milk from those big stores which will deliver in rural areas. It is small wonder that tinned milk is more often drunk than fresh in the villages surrounded by dairy cattle. But the big distributors have won handsomely everywhere.

The latest milk regulations have not cured this, but intensified it. (1) The small man who had four cows until lately was able to supply his neighbour.

[1] This was encouraged in the past by the big distributors who wanted to beat down the natural liquid milk farmers close to their market. But the distributors found it a boomerang and so they gained more by the Milk Board's control of retail prices and manufactured milk than the farmers.

Now he is ruled out. (2) The exclusion of Grade
"A" T.T. producers from the original scheme
left the pioneers of clean milk production untouched, and so made it more remunerative for
really high-class milk to be produced; they did not
have to pay the levy amounting to twopence and
sometimes threepence a gallon so that the milk
going into manufacture could receive a liquid price
subsidy. Here again was the germ of a first-rate
national milk supply and of real co-operation by the
producers of first-rate milk. If this had gone on it
would gradually have broken the Milk Board except as a market for second-rate milk and manufac-
turing supplies. Thus an organic organization of
good liquid milk producers might have been built
up. When the levy has been paid to the Milk
Board, the Grade "A" T.T. producer in future
will receive little more for his milk than the
ordinary liquid milk producer before the Board
came into existence.

The cost of Grade "A" T.T. milk is such, including cowshed regulations, that it can no longer pay
the farmer to produce it under these circumstances
when he is at the mercy of the well-intentioned but
ignorant bureaucrats of the Ministry of Health.
However conscientious a Ministry of Health inspector may be, he can only go on the written
instructions for regulations of his Ministry, which
are without regard to the realities of clean milk
production, since these regulations are based on a
discreditable if not yet discredited urban worship

of "bugs" and plumbing. (3) If he goes in for an attested herd, unless he is a specialized milk farmer,[1] he will have the fantastic business of having to test his pigs and sheep, lest his precious cows might get tuberculosis out of the air and off the broad pastures, and all this for one penny per gallon extra. In spite of this business of accredited herds, testing and cowshed regulations, most of the milk so produced will be bulked with the less clean milk, thoroughly mixed and then pasteurized. (4) Last in the milk regulations we come to the supreme folly of local option for compulsory pasteurization. Thus in spite of appearances we have put a premium on dirty milk and irresponsibility in production. Compulsory pasteurization will deprive those who want good raw milk of the opportunity of getting it, and it will drive the remaining producer-retailers and the small local distributors out of the market; all this entirely for the benefit of the big combines, though nominally for the safety of those who cannot resist germs in milk, which are in existence all about them in any case.

No co-operation has ever been successful unless it is built up from the bottom like the pre-war Irish organization, and it can never last unless the distributor is either controlled by the producer or is part of his organization. No milk production can be sound unless it pays, in those parts of the country suited to it, to manufacture butter and

[1] Specialized farming is a danger to the balance and fertility of the land.

R   257

cheese, and no intensive pig production can be truly economical and healthy unless skim milk is a daily part of the pigs' ration. So we see that the Government over pigs and milk have made almost every mistake it is possible to make. Over half of England's area pigs and milk should be the basis of our agriculture both on arable and grass land.

Now we come to the purely arable part of the Government's policy. So far it has been concerned with sugar-beet, potatoes and wheat. The wrong method of restriction of potato acreage has already been discussed. Sugar-beet was subsidized in the beginning very largely to the benefit of foreign factories which have regained their capital from the subsidies. Sugar-beet has been treated for the farmer as a profit-making crop when it should have been merely a method of cleaning the land by deep cultivation at no cost, since the crop should have just paid for itself in ordinary years. But because it has been one of the few arable crops to pay it has been used as a cash crop too often in some rotations, and has been forced with artificial manure to the detriment of the land. Wheat likewise by the quota system has been the only cereal crop for which there was a certain market. Here again, wheat has been forced to the detriment of the land since it has been grown too often without dung or sheep-folding beforehand.

Now we have a new order guaranteeing oat- and barley-growing so that other parts of England may have a share in cereal subsidies, but as only one crop in each season can get the subsidy on any particular farm this will do nothing to improve the standard of arable farming, which should be the only excuse for subsidy of this type. Fertility will not come back in this way, and farming returns will not be more prosperous except in non-wheat-growing districts. It is right to provide for a low but reasonable minimum price for cereal crops,[1] as indeed for all products of the farm. But the only way to ensure fertility is to subsidize the root brake for sheep and cattle; or at least to subsidize the production of short wool which comes from arable sheep, and to subsidize the winter yard-fed bullock more heavily than the grass-fed bullock of summer and autumn. At last the beef subsidy is beginning to increase beef production, but it makes no such seasonal distinction in favour of fertility.

Finally, we come to the Minister's specific proposals to deal with fertility by subsidizing lime and basic slag. Mr. Morrison has made history by being the first Minister to conceive that help to agriculture should begin with the soil. Both these proposals are excellent but they are not fundamental. Lime is excellent to neutralize acidity in the ground, just as bicarbonate of soda is excellent to neutralize acidity in the stomach, but they do not cure the causes of acidity, which is bad farming in one case and unwise eating in the other. The German peasant has a saying that lime makes rich

[1] See the literature of the Rural Reconstruction Association on "the just price".

fathers but poor sons. He means that lime can cover up a multitude of sins which take a generation to become apparent on the land. Lime does good but it is not essential, speaking generally, if the humus content of the soil is high and its general balance in cropping is preserved. In England nearly every essential plant requirement is present—*provided the soil is in a sufficiently healthy state for the plant to use it*. And in nearly every case, if all organic refuse is returned to the soil together with bone manure and where possible seaweed manure, there need never be any necessity to use artificial manure as the intensive agriculture of the East has shown us for over four thousand years. Therefore, liming may very likely become only an expedient and a substitute for balanced high farming. The same thing applies to basic slag, which with lime are probably the most innocuous inorganic manures. Basic slag does improve pasture for eight to fifteen years but after that records as to its value are curiously silent. Basic slag, like lime, will be useless unless something is done simultaneously to increase the livestock and to bring back balanced farming. If there is not enough livestock, slag will only mean that it will be easier for the farmer to sell more fodder crops off the land, which is the basis of bankruptcy for the next generation.

In this connection mention is made of research in grass-drying to use up the extra fodder, for sale presumably, and to lessen the imports of feeding stuffs, which is an admirable thing in itself. But if grass-drying is proved successful and economic only on a large scale, it will provide a dangerous temptation to specialize in grass-drying ranches using artificial manures to produce larger crops for sale to other farmers. This too would prove to be the most undesirable type of farming. The only grass-drying—it would be very valuable then—which would be sound, is one which made it possible for the ordinary farmer to dry a certain proportion of his grass and green fodder crops every year, in an elastic rotation. This would indeed provide concentrated food, avoid risks of wet weather and clean both grass and arable fields. In fact, if this system was well established, the productivity of our land could be so increased, that, with extra crops of oats and roots, we need import no concentrated foodstuffs in an average season. But it must be remembered that used wrongly, by cutting the same acreage twice or more each year and for year after year, it would mean the ruin of the land.

The Government propose also to give a very large grant for veterinary research in disease. This money will be wasted unless it is conducted for research in how to keep animals healthy. If it is conducted on the lines of ordinary medical research, like cancer and influenza research, to name two striking examples, it will only serve to make men overlook the cause of disease. Virus' serum and bacterial cultures may enable men to shirk the results of wrong living; they do not cure morbidity. If the present medical practice for man and animal continue, most men and animals will soon be no more than subnormal walking museums of bacteriological cultures. After experience in the tuberculin-testing of some thousands of cattle and of other forms of injection, the writer is convinced that we are making a bogey of disease, which would cause no serious harm if we bred and fed animals aright on well-farmed land. The approach to disease is done by the minds of men who see so much disease that they forget to observe health or consider the causes of health.

Admirable as the Royal College of Veterinary Surgeons may be, it is placed in a town and is not connected with the soil. It is in danger of proving useful mainly for prolonging the vicious little lives of pets belonging to the photographed classes. It has no opportunity to find out the sources of health since it is divorced from the soil. Obviously so bald a statement does not do justice to the fine minds of the men responsible for the College, but it does indicate the pitfalls in their path.

The greatest piece of research which the Government could encourage would be to see that certain areas which were farmed properly were self-supporting in all foods for animals as well as in manuring; that these areas then should feed either the local schools or else a certain given proportion of the population. The results on man and crop and animal would give more data for future policy than anything else. Schools would be particularly valuable, as in this case the cooking could be supervised,

262

and the surrounding neighbourhood and the holiday periods would be the controls by which to judge.

In addition the question of pasteurization should be properly gone into in the effects on teeth and bone, and in the case of young animals in the effects of after life, including fecundity. The health of soil and crop and animal is the first consideration in man's health; the research station in crop-growing and veterinary science is in an integral part of human medicine.[1]

The effects of housing cattle and pigs on concrete, the difference between intensive indoor methods and outdoor methods should be observed. T.B. is not a terrible disease even by present statistics of mortality, but it would become only the heritage of those who have not the stamina to survive, if we were to live properly and forget microbe worship. This applies equally to animal and man.

Research in health might make and should make all these modern microbe phobias a bad dream of these days of false standards. Research should also be conducted on the right use of land and varieties, so as to observe the resistance of plants, trees, and small fruit to pests, when these are grown on suitable ground with good organic manure. If disease

---

[1] See Dr. G. Arbour Stephen's letter to the *Morning Post* of August 31st, 1937, wherein he states that the Green Cross Institute nurses in Hungary have to be well-versed in the problems of agriculture.

is deliberately introduced to these and if control plots of poison-sprayed land are set side by side to judge by, we may have another aspect of health and economy from which to learn.

We are on the edge of rediscovering many ancient truths in the world of husbandry which we have lost in the exigencies of modern practice; we should not despise research in the interactive effects of different plants and trees on other crops, nor the effect of the moon on growth and decay. The old peasant lore is not fairy tales but the results of thousands of centuries of observation which now requires explanation. If we learn and act on all these things the people will have health; and the farmer will have a new and ancient world of wisdom open to him:

> ". . . so shall he make his gain
> And please his fields."[1]

[1] V. Sackville West, *The Land*.

INDEX

265

Merchant shipping, foreign
 owned, 32, 33
—— —— shortage of per-
  sonnel, 33, 34
Milk, home production, 130,
 183, 252–258
—— Marketing Board, 252–
 258
—— skim, 130
Milk and Dairy Order, 125
Milling, advantages of inland, 67
Monoculture, evil effects of,
 102, 200
Morrison, Mr., 259
Mussolini, Signor, 21, 62,
 89, 102
Mutton, home production,
 132
—— imports, 24, 135, 213

Nations, League of, 21
Navy, British, 34–39
—— —— need for person-
 nel, 37
New Zealand, 24, 99, 144,
 202, 225, 230, 231
Nickel, 213
Nutrition, importance of adequate, 71–87, 154–157

Oats, 134, 214, 258
—— imports, 214
Oil fuel, 27, 28, 29, 41
—— Empire supplies of, 28
—— imports of, 29, 214

Oriental farming, 138, 139
Overseas investments, 225

Panama Canal, 24
Paper, 214
Pasteurization, 257, 263
Pasture, 173, 174
Peas, 134, 135
Persia, 105
Petroleum imports, 214
Pfeiffer, Dr., 159, 181
Pigs, 130, 131
—— cottage, 217
—— saving in imports, 131,
 135
Poland, 238, 239
Policies, agricultural, 45, 49,
 50, 247–264
—— —— in war, 45
—— —— Government,
 247–264
Population, Great Britain, 30,
 39, 77, 189–191
—— Empire, 201–204
Pork, home production, 183
Potato Board, 175
Potatoes, 53, 128, 134, 175,
 176
Poultry, 160, 190
—— development, 132, 133,
 183

Rainfall, 129, 160, 162
Rearmament, 45, 248
Research, 260–264
Rice, 214
Roads, Arterial, 110